EVERYDAY EXPRESS

Delicious food for the family ready in under **60 MINUTES**

PUBLISHED IN 2017 BY BOUNTY BOOKS BASED ON MATERIALS LICENSED TO IT BY BAUER MEDIA BOOKS, AUSTRALIA.

BAUER MEDIA BOOKS ARE PUBLISHED BY
BAUER MEDIA PTY LIMITED
54 PARK ST, SYDNEY; GPO BOX 4088,
SYDNEY, NSW 2001 AUSTRALIA
PHONE +61 2 9282 8618; FAX +61 2 9126 3702
WWW.AWWCOOKBOOKS.COM.AU

PUBLISHER
JO RUNCIMAN

EDITORIAL & FOOD DIRECTOR
PAMELA CLARK

DIRECTOR OF SALES, MARKETING & RIGHTS
BRIAN CEARNES

CREATIVE DIRECTOR
HANNAH BLACKMORE

DESIGNERS
MENG KOACH, JEANNEL CUNANAN

SENIOR EDITOR
STEPHANIE KISTNER

JUNIOR EDITOR
AMANDA LEES

FOOD EDITOR
REBECCA MELI

OPERATIONS MANAGER
DAVID SCOTTO

PRINTED IN CHINA
BY LEO PAPER PRODUCTS LTD

PUBLISHED AND DISTRIBUTED IN THE
UNITED KINGDOM BY BOUNTY BOOKS,
A DIVISION OF OCTOPUS PUBLISHING GROUP LTD
CARMELITE HOUSE
50 VICTORIA EMBANKMENT
LONDON, EC4Y 0DZ
UNITED KINGDOM
INFO@OCTOPUS-PUBLISHING.CO.UK;
WWW.OCTOPUSBOOKS.CO.UK

INTERNATIONAL FOREIGN LANGUAGE RIGHTS
BRIAN CEARNES, BAUER MEDIA BOOKS
BCEARNES@BAUER-MEDIA.COM.AU

A CATALOGUE RECORD FOR THIS BOOK IS
AVAILABLE FROM THE BRITISH LIBRARY.

ISBN: 978-0-7537-3235-9

EVERYDAY
EXPRESS
Delicious food for the family ready in under 60 MINUTES
Bounty
Books

Contents

FAST *family*

OUR MODERN LIVES ARE BECOMING INCREASINGLY PACKED WITH AFTER-WORK ACTIVITIES AND OBLIGATIONS THAT KEEP US BUSY AND OUT OF THE KITCHEN. BUT CREATING HOMEMADE NUTRITIOUS FOOD THAT EVEN THE KIDS WILL SCOFF DOWN DOESN'T NEED TO BE DIFFICULT. WITH OUR RECIPES YOU'LL BE ABLE TO WHIP UP ANYTHING, FROM A DELICIOUS LUNCHBOX TO A HEARTY DINNER, IN A FLASH.

SPEEDY FAMILY MEALS

Making healthy and filling food for children is forefront on everyone's mind these days. But not everyone has the spare time to dedicate hours in the kitchen. This is where the Australian Women's Weekly Test Kitchen comes in. With a chapter on lunchbox ideas, weeknight dinners, slightly more involved weekend meals and quick and satisfying sweet treats, you can deliver homemade meals to your family 7 days a week.

COOKING FOR KIDS

Children can be the pickiest eaters, and it can be a struggle for many parents to cook a variety of meals that their kids will actually finish. But getting your children to eat new food is at the core of them being healthy, active eaters. Our recipes are designed to appeal to the entire family, using fresh ingredients (with helpful shortcuts) to make sure your family is enjoying the best of what is available. All recipes avoid chilli and other strong herbs and spices that may upset a young palate, while maintaining a variety of ingredients and flavour.

ALLERGIES AND INTOLERANCES

It's a reality of life that there are a vast number of restrictions in what people are able to eat decided by their individual intolerances and allergies. We have helpfully labelled many of our recipes that are dairy- or gluten-free, so that you can be safe in the dinner choices you make. We have also labelled those which contain no meat, to allow you to introduce more vegetarian meals to your weekly dinner plans.

IN YOUR TROLLEY

There are an abundance of products now available from your local supermarket that make preparing and cooking wholesome meals easier than ever before. Healthy alternatives to highly processed pre-packaged foods are filling the shelves, as people become more aware of the long lasting effects of eating preservatives and sugar-filled snack foods. Also packaged foods are required to clearly mark if the product contains any allergens, such as dairy, gluten, nuts and eggs. Make use of convenience products to speed up your cooking process, without feeling guilty that you are not providing quality food to your family. Ready-cooked rice is nutritionally equal to rice cooked from scratch, so too are ready-made sauces like pesto and hummus. Sometimes all you need to transform a meal from bland to brilliant is a simple marinade or dressing. Learn to read the nutritional information on the back of all packages, and you will soon learn what's the best to feed your family and what you can leave behind on the shelf.

BUTCHERS & FISHMONGERS

A lot of butchers do a fantastic selection of marinated, trimmed, crumbed, skewered and diced meats, which help cut down on preparation times. If you can't find what you're looking for, ask the butcher to trim and dice the meat so it's ready for cooking. Seafood is a nutritious and healthy meal option, but takes time to clean, fillet and shell. Most fishmongers are happy to do these jobs for you, and usually sell filleted fish, shelled prawns and marinara mixes. Prepared seafood is readily available at most supermarkets.

IN THE KITCHEN

Take advantage of kitchen utensils to speed up food preparation. Implementing a good system in the kitchen makes it much easier to work quickly and multi-task. Some of the Test Kitchen's favourite tools include a V-slicer or a mandoline, food processor, blender, sharp knives, scissors, a sharp vegetable peeler and a really sharp grater. Electrical appliances such as pressure cookers and microwaves are a great help in completing each step faster, either cooking potatoes, defrosting meat or in the case of the pressure cooker, making the perfect risotto, soup or stew. Make your kitchen do the heavy lifting.

STOCK THE PANTRY

A clean, organised pantry helps you find items quickly. Opened items should be at the front of the cupboard so they are at hand when needed. Mark the date on packets, so you know when it's time to discard them. Aim to have a selection of staples, such as canned beans, tomatoes and tuna on hand. Keep a selection of condiments as these are the flavour builders of a meal – Asian sauces, spices, mustards, vinegars and oils are a must.

BULK SHOP WEEKLY

Save time by doing a regular bulk shop. Highly perishable items, such as fish, need to be purchased close to

ORGANISE THE KITCHEN

The easiest way to ensure that you cook fast is to plan ahead, know your recipe and have your workspace organised. Read your recipe from start to finish, before even picking up a knife, to understand its flow and the ingredients you will need. It is often best to lay out your ingredients, in the order that you will need them, doing any trimming or slicing as necessary. Take out pots, pans and other equipment needed for the recipe. Fill the kettle and get it boiling, ready to pour into the pan. Preheat the oven or grill or heat oil in the frying pan. Doing a little preparation like this can cut out much of the fussing, so you can concentrate on the food itself.

IN SEASON, READILY AVAILABLE FRESH INGREDIENTS ARE GREAT FOR BUDGET CONSCIOUS COOKS.

ALL INGREDIENTS USED IN THE RECIPE ARE GLUTEN-FREE AND SO FINE FOR THOSE WHO CANNOT EAT GLUTEN.

THIS BUTTON TAKES ALL THE GUESS WORK OUT OF TRYING TO FIND FAST, HEALTHY FOOD CHOICES.

NO DAIRY IS PRESENT– HOWEVER IF USING PRE-PACKAGED FOOD, BE SURE TO READ THE LABEL CAREFULLY.

NOT JUST FOR MONDAYS – MEAT-FREE IS A GREAT WAY TO START EATING MORE FRESH VEGIES.

PREPARATION

Ensure the kitchen is always stocked; dedicate one day a week to preparing a realistic weekly menu and shopping list. This sounds like a hassle, but if you set aside the time you can make sure you are not pressed to think of what to cook after a busy and tiring day. Sunday is often a good day for full-time workers to plan next week's menu. Planning your shopping helps reduce waste as well, stopping impulse purchases and buying duplicate ingredients. You will be surprised at the savings you'll make.

the time of cooking, however, it's great to buy large amounts of dry groceries fortnightly or monthly to ensure the pantry is always stocked with commonly used ingredients. Keep a chart of seasonal fruit and vegetables handy – this produce is usually available at a cheaper price as it's fresh and in plentiful supply. Make a note on your computer or smart phone of those items you frequently purchase, so you never forget everyday needs. Check the pantry first and compile a grocery list, grouping similar ingredients.

PASSING ON THE PASSION

Any recipe can become 'express' with good planning and skilful preparation. As you develop these skills, you are also teaching your children through example, how to cook and eat healthy food every day. Include your kids in the cooking process, giving them simple preparation tasks such as washing the vegetables or getting the dry ingredients out of the cupboard, to help them on their own food-loving journey. With a little practice and care, you'll have dinner on the table in no time at all.

EXPRESS LUNCH BOXES

Green TURKEY WRAPS

PREP & COOK TIME 30 MINUTES SERVES 4

1 tablespoon olive oil

1 small kumara (orange sweet potato) (250g), cut into 1cm (½-inch) rounds

1 small avocado (200g), sliced thinly

1 tablespoon lemon juice

200g (6½ ounces) shaved turkey breast

2 small tomatoes (180g), sliced thinly

1 small carrot (70g), cut into matchsticks

1 lebanese cucumber (130g), cut into matchsticks

½ small red onion (50g), sliced thinly

12 baby cos (romaine) lettuce leaves

green tahini

¼ cup (70g) tahini

2 tablespoons fresh flat-leaf parsley leaves

2 tablespoons lemon juice

1 tablespoon olive oil

1 small clove garlic, crushed

1 Make green tahini.
2 Heat the oil in a large non-stick frying pan over low heat; cook kumara, turning, for 8 minutes or until tender.
3 Place avocado and juice in a small bowl; toss to coat, drain.
4 Divide avocado, kumara, turkey, tomato, carrot, cucumber and onion into lettuce leaves. Drizzle with green tahini and roll lettuce around fillings to enclose, just before serving.
green tahini Stir ingredients until smooth; season to taste. Add a little water, if mixture is too thick.

tips You will need about 1 or 2 baby cos (romaine) lettuce, depending on their size. Transport the filled lettuce wraps and green tahini packed separately; drizzle with the green tahini just before serving.

Gluten
FREE

Meat
FREE

Capsicum & ricotta FRITTATA

PREP & COOK TIME 40 MINUTES **SERVES** 8

- **8 eggs**
- **¼ cup (60ml) milk**
- **⅓ cup (40g) coarsely grated cheddar**
- **¼ cup small fresh basil leaves**
- **100g (3 ounces) firm fresh ricotta**
- **1 medium red capsicum (bell pepper) (200g), sliced thinly**
- **1 medium green capsicum (bell pepper) (200g), sliced thinly**

1 Preheat oven to 220°C/425°F.
2 Whisk eggs, milk and cheddar in a large jug; season.
3 Heat oiled 17cm (6¾-inch) (base measurement) ovenproof frying pan over medium heat. Add egg mixture to pan; cook, about 3 minutes, scraping edges of egg into centre of pan. Top with basil, ricotta and capsicum. Cook frittata, without stirring, over medium heat, for 2 minutes or until base and edges are almost set. Transfer pan to oven; bake frittata, uncovered, for 15 minutes or until set and browned lightly. Stand in pan 5 minutes.
4 Slide frittata onto serving plate; cut into eight pieces.

tips You need a frying pan with an ovenproof handle for this recipe, or cover the handle with a few layers of foil to protect it from the heat of the oven. The frittata can be eaten hot, warm or at room temperature.

Tomato chutney & HAM MUFFINS

PREP & COOK TIME 30 MINUTES (PLUS STANDING) **MAKES** 18

¼ cup (40g) polenta

¼ cup (60ml) milk

¾ cup (110g) self-raising flour

¼ cup (80g) tomato chutney

¼ cup (30g) coarsely grated cheddar

100g (3 ounces) shaved light ham, chopped coarsely

2 green onions (scallions), sliced thinly

60g (2 ounces) butter, melted

1 egg, beaten lightly

9 cherry tomatoes (180g), halved

1 Preheat oven to 180°C/350°F. Oil 18 holes of two 12-hole (1-tablespoon/20ml) mini muffin pans.

2 Combine polenta and milk in a small bowl; cover, stand for 20 minutes.

3 Sift flour into a medium bowl; stir in chutney, cheddar, ham and onion. Add melted butter, egg and polenta mixture; season. Mix until just combined. Divide mixture between pan holes. Top each muffin with a tomato half.

4 Bake muffins about 15 minutes. Stand muffins in pan 5 minutes before turning, top-side up, onto a wire rack to cool.

serving suggestion Serve with extra tomato chutney.

Cheap
EAT

Gluten
FREE

Char-grilled vegies & PUMPKIN DIP WRAPS

PREP TIME 10 MINUTES **MAKES** 4

2 x 280g (9-ounce) jars char-grilled vegetables

200g (8-ounce) tub gluten-free, dairy-free moroccan pumpkin dip

4 gluten-free wraps (200g)

40g (1½ ounces) baby rocket (arugula) leaves

1 Drain char-grilled vegetables; pat dry with paper towel, season to taste.

2 Spread pumpkin dip onto wraps; top with char-grilled vegetables and rocket leaves. Roll to enclose fillings.

tip You could use your favourite brand of gluten-free rolls instead of wraps, if you prefer.

Roast beef & COLESLAW ROLLS

PREP TIME 10 MINUTES **SERVES** 4

⅓ cup (100g) mayonnaise
⅓ cup (95g) yoghurt
1 cup (80g) finely shredded red cabbage
1 cup (80g) finely shredded green cabbage
1 medium carrot (120g), grated coarsely
1 shallot (25g), sliced thinly
¼ cup loosely packed lamb's tongue (mâche) leaves
250g (8 ounces) sliced roast beef (see tip)
4 medium multigrain bread rolls (200g), split

1 Whisk mayonnaise with yoghurt in a large bowl until combined. Mix in cabbage, carrot, shallot and lamb's tongue. Season to taste.

2 Sandwich coleslaw and beef between rolls.

tip We used sliced rare roast beef from the deli. You can use shaved ham or turkey or flaked hot smoked trout instead, if you prefer.

Chicken, mushroom & ZUCCHINI CAKES

PREP & COOK TIME 50 MINUTES **MAKES** 12

¼ cup (60ml) olive oil

100g (3 ounces) sliced swiss brown mushrooms

1 small brown onion (80g), chopped finely

3 eggs

¾ cup (110g) self-raising flour

¾ cup (90g) grated cheddar

¼ cup finely chopped fresh flat-leaf parsley

2 teaspoons finely chopped fresh thyme

1 medium zucchini (120g), grated coarsely

150g (4½ ounces) barbecued chicken, chopped finely

1 Preheat oven to 180°C/350°F. Grease a 12-hole (⅓-cup/80ml) muffin pan.

2 Heat 2 teaspoons of the oil in a large frying pan over medium-high heat; cook mushrooms, stirring occasionally, until browned lightly and tender. Remove from pan; cool.

3 Heat another 2 teaspoons of the oil in same pan; cook onion, stirring, for 3 minutes or until softened. Remove from pan; cool.

4 Whisk eggs in a large bowl; add sifted flour, cheddar, 2 tablespoons of the oil and herbs, mix well. Add mushrooms, onion, zucchini and chicken; mix well. Season. Divide mixture among prepared holes.

5 Bake cakes about 20 minutes. Stand in pan 5 minutes before turning, top-side up, onto a wire rack to cool.

serving suggestion Serve with tomato chutney.

tips Cool cakes before packing in airtight containers; cakes will keep, refrigerated, for up to 2 days. Cakes can also be frozen. Pack a frozen cake in the lunchbox in the morning and it will be thawed by lunchtime.

Loaded pepperoni
PIZZA SCROLLS

Cheap
EAT

1

2

3

4

Loaded pepperoni PIZZA SCROLLS

PREP & COOK TIME 40 MINUTES **MAKES** 9

- **2 cups (300g) self-raising flour**
- **½ teaspoon bicarbonate of soda (baking soda)**
- **1 teaspoon salt**
- **50g (1½ ounces) cold butter, chopped coarsely**
- **¾ cup (180ml) buttermilk, approximately**
- **2 tablespoons pizza sauce**
- **2 tablespoons barbecue sauce**
- **½ small red onion (50g), sliced thinly**
- **½ small green capsicum (bell pepper) (75g), sliced thinly**
- **100g (3 ounces) sliced pepperoni, chopped coarsely**
- **½ cup (100g) well-drained pineapple pieces, chopped coarsely (see tips)**
- **⅓ cup (55g) drained sliced kalamata olives**
- **1 cup (120g) pizza cheese**

1 Preheat oven to 200°C/400°F. Oil a shallow 22cm (9-inch) square cake pan.

2 Sift flour, soda and salt into a medium bowl; rub in butter. Add enough buttermilk to mix to a soft, sticky dough. Turn dough onto floured surface; knead lightly until smooth. Roll dough into a 30cm x 40cm (12-inch x 16-inch) rectangle.

3 Spread dough with combined sauces; sprinkle with onion, capsicum, pepperoni, pineapple, olives and half the cheese. Roll dough tightly from long side. Using serrated knife, trim ends. Cut roll into 9 slices; place scrolls, cut-side up, in pan. Sprinkle with remaining cheese. Bake about 25 minutes.

tips We drained our pineapple and then patted it dry on paper towels to prevent the pineapple making the scrolls soggy. These scrolls are delicious eaten warm or cold. For a meat-free verison, replace the pepperoni with thinly sliced swiss brown mushrooms.

Best-ever chicken SALAD SANDWICHES

PREP TIME 20 MINUTES **MAKES** 4

- **1½ cups (240g) shredded barbecued chicken**
- **1 small carrot (70g), grated coarsely**
- **125g (4 ounces) canned creamed corn**
- **¼ cup (65g) soft ricotta**
- **2 tablespoons whole-egg mayonnaise**
- **1 tablespoon finely chopped fresh chives**
- **8 slices wholemeal bread (360g)**
- **40g (1 ounce) butter, softened**
- **¼ small iceberg lettuce, sliced thinly**

1 Combine chicken, carrot, corn, ricotta, mayonnaise and chives in a medium bowl; season to taste.

2 Spread bread with butter; sandwich lettuce and chicken mixture between bread slices. Cut the sandwiches however you like.

tips You can spread the bread with smashed avocado instead of butter, if you prefer; add a little lemon juice to the avocado smash to prevent it discolouring in the lunchbox. For a dairy-free option, use your favourite dairy-free spread or avocado instead of butter and drop the ricotta and increase the mayonnaise slightly.

Healthy CHOICE

Cheap
EAT

Wheaty banana & CRANBERRY LOAVES

PREP & COOK TIME 40 MINUTES (PLUS COOLING) **MAKES** 8

1 medium banana (200g)
1 tablespoon lemon juice
1½ cups (225g) self-raising flour
½ cup (110g) firmly packed light brown sugar
1 cup (100g) crushed Weet-Bix
⅓ cup (45g) dried cranberries
1 cup (280g) mashed banana (see tips)
½ cup (125ml) buttermilk
80g (2½ ounces) butter, melted
1 egg, beaten lightly

honey icing

1 tablespoon honey
2 teaspoons milk
½ cup (80g) icing (confectioners') sugar

1 Preheat oven to 180°C/350°F. Grease an 8-hole (¾-cup/180ml) mini loaf pan; line each pan hole with a strip of baking paper.

2 Thickly slice banana lengthways; cut slices in half crossways. Combine with juice in a medium bowl.

3 Sift flour and sugar into a large bowl; stir in Weet-Bix, cranberries and mashed banana. Add buttermilk, butter and egg; stir only until mixture is just combined. Divide mixture between pan holes; top with banana slices.

4 Bake about 25 minutes. Stand loaves in pan 5 minutes before turning, top-side up, onto a wire rack to cool.

5 Make honey icing. Spoon icing over cold loaves; stand until set.

honey icing Combine honey and milk in a small saucepan; stir over low heat until combined. Remove from heat; gradually stir in sifted icing sugar.

tips You will need 2 large (460g) overripe bananas to make 1 cup mashed banana. Uniced loaves can be frozen for up to 3 months.

Lamb, kumara & CHICKPEA SALAD

PREP & COOK TIME 30 MINUTES **SERVES** 4

- **2 medium kumara (orange sweet potato) (800g), chopped coarsely**
- **1 tablespoon olive oil**
- **400g (12½ ounces) lamb backstraps (eye of loin)**
- **400g (12½ ounces) canned chickpeas (garbanzo beans), drained, rinsed**
- **1 small red onion (100g), sliced thinly**
- **150g (4½ ounces) baby spinach leaves**
- **100g (3 ounces) fetta, crumbled**

lemon and cranberry vinaigrette

- **1 clove garlic, crushed**
- **2 teaspoons finely grated lemon rind**
- **¼ cup (60ml) olive oil**
- **2 tablespoons white wine vinegar**
- **2 tablespoons dried cranberries**

1 Preheat oven to 200°C/400°F.

2 Combine kumara and oil in a large roasting pan; season. Roast for 15 minutes or until tender.

3 Meanwhile, season lamb; cook on a heated oiled grill plate (or barbecue or grill) over medium-high heat, for 4 minutes each side or until cooked as desired. Remove from heat; cover, rest 5 minutes. Slice lamb thinly.

4 Make lemon and cranberry vinaigrette.

5 Place kumara in a large bowl with lamb, chickpeas, onion, spinach and vinaigrette; toss gently to combine. Serve salad sprinkled with fetta.

lemon and cranberry vinaigrette Place ingredients in a screw-top jar; shake well. Season to taste.

tips Transport salad and dressing separately, in airtight containers; dress salad just before serving. Substitute the lamb with some shredded leftover roast or barbecued chicken or some quartered hard-boiled eggs, if you prefer.

Chicken, corn & chive
MINI QUICHES

PREP & COOK TIME 40 MINUTES **MAKES** 12

- **2 eggs**
- **1 tablespoon pouring cream**
- **2 sheets shortcrust pastry**
- **125g (4 ounces) finely shredded barbecued chicken**
- **125g (4 ounces) drained canned corn kernels**
- **2 tablespoons finely chopped fresh chives**
- **¼ cup (20g) finely grated parmesan**

1 Preheat oven to 180°C/350°F. Grease a 12-hole (2-tablespoon/40ml) flat-based patty pan.
2 Whisk eggs with cream in a medium jug; season.
3 Using a 7cm (3-inch) cutter, cut 12 rounds from pastry; press rounds into pan holes. Divide chicken, corn and chives between pastry cases. Top with egg mixture. Sprinkle with parmesan. Bake about 25 minutes or until quiches are set and pastry is browned lightly.

tips These quiches are perfect served warm or cold. This is a great way to use up leftover roasted or barbecued chicken. You can use whatever filling ingredients you like; try replacing the chicken with chopped ham and the corn with frozen peas. You could also use gluten-free shortcrust pastry (available in most large supermarkets, in the freezer section).

Tuna & olive BAGUETTES

PREP TIME 10 MINUTES **MAKES** 4

2 x 30cm (12-inch) baguettes

⅓ cup (80g) whole-egg mayonnaise

425g (13½ ounces) canned tuna in oil, drained, flaked

⅓ cup (50g) seeded kalamata olives, sliced

1 large tomato (220g), sliced thickly

½ small red onion (50g), sliced thinly

1 lebanese cucumber (130g), cut into ribbons

2 tablespoons micro basil leaves

1 Split bread open without cutting all the way through. Spread cut-sides of bread with mayonnaise.

2 Sandwich tuna, olives, tomato, onion, cucumber and basil in bread.

3 Cut each baguette in half. Serve cut into smaller pieces, if you prefer.

tip You can use your favourite gluten-free bread or wraps, if you like.

Dairy
FREE

Meat
FREE

Vegie & chickpea FRITTERS

PREP & COOK TIME 30 MINUTES **MAKES** 16

400g (12½ ounces) canned chickpeas (garbanzo beans), drained, rinsed

¾ cup (110g) wholemeal self-raising flour

½ cup (125ml) milk

2 eggs

1 cup (160g) frozen peas, corn and capsicum mix, thawed

2 green onions (scallions), sliced thinly

1 small zucchini (90g), grated coarsely

1 small carrot (70g), grated coarsely

½ cup (60g) coarsely grated cheddar

2 tablespoons coarsely chopped fresh mint leaves

1 Blend or process chickpeas until chopped coarsely.
2 Sift flour into medium bowl; add any husks from wheat to bowl. Make a well in centre of flour; stir in combined milk and eggs until smooth. Stir in chickpeas, pea, corn and capsicum mix, onion, zucchini, carrot, cheddar and mint; season.
3 Drop ¼ cup batter for each fritter, in batches, into a heated oiled large frying pan (allow room for mixture to spread). Cook, over medium heat, about 5 minutes or until fritters are browned lightly both sides and cooked through.

serving suggestion Serve with tomato chutney and mixed salad leaves.
tips These fritters are delicious eaten warm or cold. Cooked fritters can be frozen, layered between sheets of baking paper, in an airtight container, for up to 3 months.

Tropical YOGHURT CUPCAKES

PREP & COOK TIME 50 MINUTES (PLUS COOLING) **MAKES** 12

90g (3 ounces) unsalted butter, softened

½ cup (110g) caster (superfine) sugar

1 teaspoon finely grated orange rind

2 eggs

1 cup (150g) self-raising flour

⅓ cup (80ml) fresh passionfruit pulp

½ cup (120g) finely chopped well-drained pineapple pieces (see tips)

⅓ cup (95g) greek-style yoghurt

cream cheese icing

30g (1 ounce) unsalted butter, softened

100g (3 ounces) cream cheese, at room temperature

1 teaspoon finely grated orange rind

1½ cups (240g) icing (confectioners') sugar

1 Preheat oven to 180°C/350°F. Line 12-hole (⅓-cup/80ml) muffin pan with paper cases or baking paper.
2 Beat butter, sugar, rind and eggs in a medium bowl with an electric mixer until light and fluffy.
3 Stir in sifted flour, passionfruit, pineapple and yoghurt. Divide mixture evenly into paper cases; smooth surface.
4 Bake cakes about 25 minutes. Stand cakes in pan 5 minutes before turning, top-side up, onto wire rack to cool.
5 Make cream cheese icing. Spread cooled cakes with icing.
cream cheese icing Beat butter, cream cheese and rind in a small bowl with electric mixer until light and fluffy; gradually beat in sifted icing sugar.

tips Drain pineapple, then spread out onto paper towel to absorb any excess moisture. Uniced cakes can be frozen for up to 3 months. Top with extra passionfruit pulp and serve as an after-school treat, or stir the pulp through the icing before using to ice the cakes. We used the pulp of 2 large passionfruit (about 2 tablespoons).

FAST MUESLI BARS

Choc-cranberry MUESLI BARS

PREP & COOK TIME 40 MINUTES (PLUS COOLING) **MAKES** 8 BARS

Preheat oven to 150°C/300°F. Grease a 20cm x 30cm (8-inch x 12-inch) rectangular slice pan; line base and long sides with baking paper, extending paper 5cm (2 inches) over sides. Combine 2½ cups puffed rice, ⅓ cup sunflower seeds, ½ cup pepitas (pumpkin seed kernels), ½ cup coarsely chopped dried cranberries and 1 tablespoon white sesame seeds in a large bowl. Place ¾ cup honey, 1 teaspoon vanilla extract and ½ teaspoon salt flakes in a small saucepan over medium heat; cook, stirring, for 2 minutes or until mixture just comes to a simmer. Pour honey mixture over dry ingredients; stir through until evenly coated. Cool for 5 minutes. Add ½ cup dark chocolate chips; stir until combined. Transfer mixture to pan; press down firmly with the back of a lightly oiled spoon. Bake about 25 minutes or until golden brown. Cool in pan. Cut into 8 bars.

Coconut fruit salad MUESLI BARS

PREP & COOK TIME 40 MINUTES (PLUS COOLING) **MAKES** 8 BARS

Preheat oven to 150°C/300°F. Grease a 20cm x 30cm (8-inch x 12-inch) rectangular slice pan; line base and long sides with baking paper, extending paper 5cm (2 inches) over sides. Combine 2½ cups puffed rice, ⅓ cup sunflower seeds, ½ cup pepitas (pumpkin seed kernels), ½ cup chopped dried fruit medley, ½ cup shredded coconut and 1 tablespoon white sesame seeds in a large bowl. Place ¾ cup honey, 1 teaspoon vanilla extract and ½ teaspoon salt flakes in a small saucepan over medium heat; cook, stirring, for 2 minutes or until mixture just comes to a simmer. Pour honey mixture over dry ingredients; stir through until evenly coated. Transfer mixture to pan; press down firmly with the back of a lightly oiled spoon. Bake about 25 minutes or until golden brown. Cool in pan. Cut into 8 bars.

Berry & white choc MUESLI BARS

PREP & COOK TIME 40 MINUTES (PLUS COOLING) **MAKES** 8 BARS

Preheat oven to 150°C/300°F. Grease a 20cm x 30cm (8-inch x 12-inch) rectangular slice pan; line base and long sides with baking paper, extending paper 5cm (2 inches) over sides. Combine 2½ cups puffed rice, ⅓ cup sunflower seeds, ½ cup pepitas (pumpkin seed kernels), ½ cup dried blueberries and 1 tablespoon white sesame seeds in a large bowl. Place ¾ cup honey, 1 teaspoon vanilla extract and ½ teaspoon salt flakes in a small saucepan over medium heat; cook, stirring, for 2 minutes or until mixture just comes to a simmer. Pour honey mixture over dry ingredients; stir through until evenly coated. Cool for 5 minutes. Add ½ cup white chocolate chips; stir until combined. Transfer mixture to pan; press down firmly with the back of a lightly oiled spoon. Bake about 25 minutes or until golden brown. Cool in pan. Cut into 8 bars.

Apple pie MUESLI BARS

PREP & COOK TIME 40 MINUTES (PLUS COOLING) **MAKES** 8 BARS

Preheat oven to 150°C/300°F. Grease a 20cm x 30cm (8-inch x 12-inch) rectangular slice pan; line base and long sides with baking paper, extending paper 5cm (2 inches) over sides. Combine 2½ cups puffed rice, ⅓ cup sunflower seeds, ½ cup pepitas (pumpkin seed kernels), ½ cup finely chopped dried apple, 1 tablespoon white sesame seeds and 1 teaspoon ground cinnamon in a large bowl. Place ¾ cup honey, 1 teaspoon vanilla extract and ½ teaspoon salt flakes in a small saucepan over medium heat; cook, stirring, for 2 minutes or until mixture just comes to a simmer. Pour honey mixture over dry ingredients; stir through until evenly coated. Transfer mixture to pan; press down firmly with the back of a lightly oiled spoon. Bake about 25 minutes or until golden brown. Cool in pan. Cut into 8 bars.

Egg, chive & spinach SANDWICH

PREP TIME 10 MINUTES **MAKES** 4

4 hard-boiled eggs, halved

2 tablespoons low-fat ricotta

⅓ cup (65g) low-fat cottage cheese

⅓ cup finely chopped fresh chives

8 slices rye bread (360g)

30g (1 ounce) baby spinach leaves

1 Place egg, cheeses and chives in a medium bowl; using a potato masher or back of a fork, crush until combined.
2 Divide egg mixture between four slices of bread; top with spinach, then with remaining bread.

tips This is the perfect portable lunch. Boil the eggs the night before and make the filling and the sandwiches in the morning. Wrap them well in plastic wrap. If you like, add in some curry powder to taste.

Spinach & FETTA STRAWS

PREP & COOK TIME 40 MINUTES **MAKES** 24

250g (8 ounces) frozen spinach, thawed

100g (3 ounces) fetta, crumbled

½ cup (40g) finely grated parmesan

2 sheets puff pastry

1 Preheat oven to 220°C/425°F. Oil oven trays; line with baking paper.

2 Place spinach in a fine sieve; squeeze excess water from spinach. Chop spinach coarsely; pat dry between sheets of absorbent paper.

3 Sprinkle half the spinach and half the combined cheeses over one pastry sheet. Top with another sheet of puff pastry; sprinkle with remaining spinach and combined cheeses. Cut pastry stack in half; place one stack on top of the other, press down firmly. Cut pastry crossways into 24 strips; twist strips, pinching ends to seal.

4 Place strips on trays. Bake about 15 minutes or until golden and crisp.

Cheap
EAT

Bacon & herb
LAMB PATTIES

PREP & COOK TIME 25 MINUTES MAKES 8

- 1 clove garlic, crushed
- 2 green onions (scallions), chopped finely
- 500g (1 pound) lean minced (ground) lamb
- 1 egg
- ¾ cup (50g) stale wholemeal breadcrumbs
- 2 tablespoons finely chopped fresh flat-leaf parsley
- 2 tablespoons finely chopped fresh oregano
- ⅓ cup (110g) tomato chutney
- 8 streaky bacon slices (200g)
- 60g (2 ounces) watercress, sprigs picked

1 Combine garlic, onion, lamb, egg, breadcrumbs, herbs and chutney in a large bowl; season well. Shape mixture into eight patties. Wrap each patty with one slice of bacon. Secure with toothpicks.

2 Cook patties in a heated oiled large frying pan, over medium heat, until browned on both sides and cooked through. Remove and discard toothpicks. Serve patties with watercress.

serving suggestion Make it a pattie roll by spreading a bread roll (or a pitta pocket or wrap) with tomato chutney or hummus and adding a sliced pattie with some salad.

tips Freeze individual cooled patties in airtight containers for up to 1 month. Thaw overnight in the fridge; reheat in microwave at work or eat at room temperature, if taking to school.

Beef & pea HAND PIES

PREP & COOK TIME 40 MINUTES **MAKES** 12

- **2 teaspoons olive oil**
- **1 small brown onion (80g), chopped finely**
- **1 clove garlic, crushed**
- **500g (1 pound) minced (ground) beef**
- **2 tablespoons tomato paste**
- **⅔ cup (170g) bottled passata**
- **½ cup (60g) frozen peas**
- **⅓ cup finely chopped fresh flat-leaf parsley**
- **3 sheets puff pastry**
- **1 egg, beaten lightly**
- **1 cup (250ml) tomato sauce (ketchup)**

1 Preheat oven to 200°C/400°F. Oil oven trays.
2 Heat oil in a large frying pan over medium-high heat; cook onion and garlic, stirring, for 3 minutes or until onion softens. Increase heat to high, add beef; cook, stirring, for 5 minutes or until beef is browned and cooked through. Add paste, passata and peas; cook, stirring, until heated through. Remove from heat; stir in parsley. Season to taste.
3 Cut each pastry sheet into quarters (you will have 12 squares). Spoon ¼ cup of beef mixture into centre of each square. Brush edges with a little egg; fold pastry in half diagonally to enclose filling, pinch edges to seal.
4 Place pies on trays; brush with egg. Bake about 15 minutes or until browned. Serve with tomato sauce.

tip Cooked pies can be frozen for up to 3 months.

Cheap
EAT

Creamy chicken & PASTA SALAD

PREP & COOK TIME 35 MINUTES **SERVES** 6

3 cups (750ml) water
400g (12½ ounces) chicken breast fillets
500g (1 pound) large pasta shells
2 sticks celery (300g), trimmed, sliced thinly
1 small red onion (100g), sliced thinly
1 cup (120g) roasted pecans
½ cup (90g) thinly sliced dill pickles
50g (1½ ounces) baby rocket (arugula) leaves

creamy tarragon dressing

¾ cup (225g) mayonnaise
½ cup (120g) sour cream
2 tablespoons lemon juice
1 tablespoon finely chopped fresh tarragon

1 Bring the water to the boil in a medium saucepan, add chicken; simmer, covered, about 10 minutes. Cool chicken in poaching liquid for 10 minutes; drain, shred coarsely.
2 Meanwhile, cook pasta in a large saucepan of boiling water until tender; drain. Rinse under cold water; drain.
3 Make creamy tarragon dressing.
4 Combine pasta in a large bowl with chicken, dressing and remaining ingredients. Season to taste.
creamy tarragon dressing Combine ingredients in a small bowl.

tips Whether you're a big kid or a little kid, this salad would also make a great dinner; so double the recipe and you've got dinner, then lunch covered for work the next day. Cornichon, French for gherkin, is a very small variety of pickled cucumber; it can be used in place of the dill pickles. If you don't like creamy dressings, you can make a simple lemon and tarragon dressing by placing ¼ cup (60ml) olive oil and ¼ cup (60ml) lemon juice and the tarragon in a screw-top jar; shake well.

Teriyaki chicken
RICE PAPER ROLLS

PREP & COOK TIME 40 MINUTES **MAKES** 24

6 chicken thigh fillets (660g)

¼ cup (60ml) thick teriyaki marinade

4 lebanese cucumbers (520g)

200g (6½ ounces) enoki mushrooms

2 teaspoons peanut oil

24 x 17cm (6¾-inch) square rice paper sheets

lime and sweet chilli dipping sauce

⅓ cup (80ml) sweet chilli sauce

2 tablespoons lime juice

1 Trim chicken and cut each fillet into eight strips lengthways. Combine chicken and marinade in a small bowl.

2 Meanwhile, cut cucumbers in half lengthways; discard seeds. Cut cucumber halves in half crossways; cut pieces into three strips lengthways. Trim enoki mushrooms.

3 Drain chicken; discard marinade. Heat oil in a large frying pan over medium-high heat; cook chicken, in batches, until cooked through. Cool 10 minutes.

4 Meanwhile, make lime and sweet chilli dipping sauce.

5 Place 1 sheet of rice paper in a medium bowl of warm water until just softened; lift sheet carefully from water, placing it on a tea-towel-covered board with a corner pointing towards you. Place two pieces of chicken horizontally in centre of rice paper; top with two pieces of cucumber then a few mushrooms. Fold the corner facing you over filling; roll rice paper to enclose filling, folding in one side after first complete turn of roll. Repeat with remaining rice paper sheets, chicken, cucumber and mushrooms. Serve rolls with dipping sauce.

lime and sweet chilli dipping sauce Combine ingredients in a small bowl.

tip Keep the rolls moist by covering them with a slightly damp piece of paper towel, then store them in an airtight container in the refrigerator.

Dairy
FREE

MID-WEEK EXPRESS

DUKKAH PRAWN SKEWERS
with labne & tomato salad

PREP & COOK TIME 30 MINUTES **SERVES** 4

1.2kg (2½ pounds) large uncooked king prawns (shrimp)

¼ cup (35g) pistachio dukkah

2 tablespoons olive oil

2 cloves garlic, crushed

2 teaspoons finely grated lemon rind

280g (9 ounces) labne

1 medium lemon (140g), cut into wedges

minty tomato salad

400g (12½ ounces) mixed baby heirloom tomatoes, chopped coarsely

1 cup loosely packed fresh flat-leaf parsley leaves

½ cup loosely packed fresh mint leaves

2 tablespoons red wine vinegar

1 tablespoon garlic oil

1 Shell and devein prawns, leaving tails intact.

2 Combine dukkah, oil, garlic and rind in a large bowl; add prawns, toss to coat in dukkah mixture.

3 Thread prawns onto 8 bamboo skewers. Cook skewers on a heated oiled grill plate (or grill or barbecue) until prawns change colour.

4 Meanwhile, make minty tomato salad.

5 Serve skewers with salad, labne and lemon wedges.

minty tomato salad Place ingredients in a large bowl; toss gently to combine. Season to taste.

tips To save time, buy already shelled and deveined prawns from your fishmonger; you will need 600g (1¼ pounds). Dukkah is found in the spice aisle of supermarkets. If your child has a nut allergy, omit the dukkah and add 2 teaspoons sumac or chopped parsley to the prawns and garlic mixture. Cover the ends of the bamboo skewers in foil to prevent scorching during cooking. Or, if you have time, soak skewers in cold water for 30 minutes.

Gluten
FREE

Healthy
CHOICE

Quinoa 'FRIED RICE'

PREP & COOK TIME 25 MINUTES (PLUS FREEZING) **SERVES** 4

1 cup (200g) white quinoa

1 tablespoon vegetable oil

4 eggs, beaten lightly

2 teaspoons sesame oil

2 cloves garlic, sliced thinly

20g (¾-ounce) piece fresh ginger, cut into matchsticks

1 medium carrot (120g), grated coarsely

1 small red capsicum (bell pepper) (150g), chopped finely

¾ cup (90g) frozen baby peas

4 green onions (scallions), sliced thinly

2 tablespoons kecap manis

½ cup loosely packed fresh coriander (cilantro) leaves

1 Cook quinoa in a large saucepan of boiling water for 12 minutes or until tender; drain. Spread quinoa on an oven tray. Freeze, uncovered, for 15 minutes.

2 Heat 1 teaspoon of the vegetable oil in a wok over high heat; pour half the egg into wok, tilt wok to make a thin omelette. Cook until set. Remove omelette from wok; roll tightly, then slice thinly. Repeat with another 1 teaspoon of the vegetable oil and remaining egg.

3 Heat remaining vegetable oil and the sesame oil in wok; add garlic, ginger, carrot and capsicum; stir-fry for 1 minute or until fragrant. Add peas and half of the green onion; stir-fry for 1 minute or until heated through.

4 Add quinoa and kecap manis; stir-fry for 1 minute or until heated through. Serve topped with omelette, coriander and remaining green onion.

tip If you have the time, cook the quinoa the day before serving, spread it over a tray and refrigerate overnight to dry it out, then continue with the recipe.

Spinach & ricotta-stuffed CHICKEN PARMIGIANA

PREP & COOK TIME 35 MINUTES **SERVES** 4

750g (1½ pounds) frozen sweet potato chips

150g (4½ ounces) baby spinach leaves

1⅓ cups (320g) ricotta

8 x 125g (4-ounce) uncrumbed chicken schnitzels

¼ cup (60ml) vegetable oil

1 cup (260g) bottled passata

1 cup (100g) coarsely grated mozzarella

2 tablespoons balsamic dressing

1 Preheat oven to 220°C/425°F.

2 Place chips on a lined oven tray; season. Cook in oven according to packet directions until golden and crisp.

3 Meanwhile, divide 40g (1½ ounces) spinach and the ricotta evenly among chicken, leaving 1cm (½-inch) border around edges. Roll up to enclose filling; secure with toothpicks.

4 Heat oil in a large frying pan over medium heat. Cook chicken, in batches, for 2 minutes each side or until golden. Remove with a slotted spoon; drain on paper towel.

5 Place chicken in an oiled shallow large baking dish; top with passata and mozzarella. Bake for 10 minutes or until cheese melts and chicken has cooked through.

6 Combine remaining spinach with dressing in a large bowl.

7 Serve chicken with kumara chips and spinach salad.

Healthy
CHOICE

Tuna & quinoa
NIÇOISE SALAD

PREP & COOK TIME 35 MINUTES **SERVES** 4

1½ cups (300g) red quinoa

4 eggs, at room temperature (see tips)

200g (6½ ounces) green beans, trimmed

425g (13½ ounces) canned tuna in oil, drained, flaked

250g (8 ounces) cherry tomatoes, halved

½ cup (60g) seeded kalamatta olives

½ cup loosely packed fresh flat-leaf parsley leaves

1 tablespoon finely chopped fresh chives

caper and parmesan vinaigrette

1 tablespoon drained baby capers, rinsed, chopped

¼ cup (20g) finely grated parmesan

¼ cup (60ml) white wine vinegar

2 tablespoons olive oil

1 small clove garlic, crushed

1 teaspoon dijon mustard

1 teaspoon caster (superfine) sugar

1 Cook quinoa in a large saucepan of boiling water for 12 minutes or until tender; drain. Set aside to cool.

2 Meanwhile, cook eggs in a small saucepan of boiling water for 8 minutes until hard-boiled. Drain; cool eggs under cold running water. Peel; halve eggs.

3 Boil, steam or microwave beans until tender; drain. Rinse under cold water; drain.

4 Meanwhile, make caper and parmesan vinaigrette.

5 Place quinoa and beans in a large bowl with tuna, tomatoes, olives, parsley and vinaigrette; toss to combine. Serve quinoa salad topped with eggs and chives.

caper and parmesan vinaigrette Combine ingredients in a small bowl; season to taste.

tips If you forget to bring the eggs to room temperature first, place them straight from the fridge into a saucepan of cold water; bring to the boil, then boil for 10 minutes. If you want to 'centre' the egg yolks, gently stir the eggs until the water comes to the boil. This filling salad would also make a great transportable lunch.

PORK SLIDERS
with apple & slaw

PREP & COOK TIME 40 MINUTES **SERVES** 6

500g (1 pound) frozen shoestring chips
600g (1¼ pounds) thick pork sausages
2 green onions (scallions), chopped finely
2 tablespoons finely chopped fresh flat-leaf parsley
¼ cup (60ml) olive oil
1 cup (100g) pizza cheese
2 small green apples (260g), sliced thinly
12 small round dinner rolls (300g), split

mint slaw

1 cup (80g) finely shredded green cabbage
¼ cup loosely packed small fresh mint leaves
1 green onion (scallion), sliced thinly on the diagonal
⅓ cup (80ml) coleslaw dressing

1 Preheat oven to 220°C/425°F.
2 Place chips on a baking-paper-lined oven tray, season; cook, in oven, according to packet directions.
3 Meanwhile, make mint slaw.
4 Remove casings from sausages; place filling in a large bowl. Add onion and parsley; mix to combine. Divide pork mixture into 12 equal portions; shape into 5cm (2-inch) patties (or same size as the bread rolls).
5 Heat half the oil in a large frying pan over medium-high heat. Add half the patties; cook 3 minutes each side. Drain on paper towel. Repeat with remaining oil and patties.
6 Remove chips from oven when ready; cover loosely to keep warm. Preheat grill (broiler) to high. Place patties on baking trays, sprinkle with cheese. Grill for 2 minutes or until cheese melts.
7 Sandwich apple, slaw and patties in rolls. Serve with chips and a green salad, if you like.
mint slaw Place ingredients in a large bowl, season to taste; toss gently to combine.

tips Use wet hands to prevent beef mixture from sticking to hands when shaping the patties. Use a toothpick to secure sliders for serving. Patties can be made a day ahead; keep covered, in the refrigerator.

PORK CUTLETS

with apple berry sauce

PREP & COOK TIME 40 MINUTES **SERVES** 4

800g (1½ pounds) kipfler (fingerling) potatoes

1 tablespoon olive oil

4 x 235g (7½-ounce) pork cutlets

40g (1½ ounces) butter

1 small red onion (100g), cut into thin wedges

1 clove garlic, crushed

1 bunch spinach (500g), trimmed, chopped coarsely

1 tablespoon apple cider vinegar

apple berry sauce

4 medium apples (600g)

40g (1½ ounces) butter

¼ cup (55g) caster (superfine) sugar

½ cup (125ml) water

125g (4 ounces) fresh or frozen raspberries

1 Make apple berry sauce.

2 Meanwhile, scrub potatoes. Prick all over with a fork. Microwave potatoes on HIGH (100%) for 2 minutes or until tender. Slice potatoes thickly.

3 Heat oil in a large frying pan over medium-high heat; season pork, cook for 4 minutes each side or until cooked as desired. Remove from pan; cover to keep warm.

4 Melt butter in same pan; cook potato, turning, for 5 minutes or until golden. Remove from pan. Reduce heat to medium; cook onion and garlic, stirring, for 3 minutes or until onion softens. Add spinach and vinegar; cook, stirring, until spinach wilts. Add potatoes; cook, stirring, until heated through. Season to taste.

5 Serve pork with spinach mixture and apple berry sauce.

apple berry sauce Peel, core and quarter apples; chop coarsely. Melt butter in a medium saucepan; cook apple, stirring, about 5 minutes or until browned lightly. Add sugar, the water and berries; cook, stirring, 5 minutes or until berries soften and sauce thickens slightly.

tip The apple berry sauce can be made a day ahead; store, covered, in the refrigerator.

Vegie PAD THAI

PREP & COOK TIME 40 MINUTES (PLUS STANDING) **SERVES** 6

200g (6½ ounces) dried rice noodles

⅓ cup (80ml) peanut oil

¼ cup (60ml) boiling water

½ cup (135g) grated palm sugar or brown sugar

1 tablespoon tamarind puree (concentrate)

¼ cup (60ml) lime juice

⅓ cup (80ml) gluten-free tamari

400g (12½ ounces) packaged fresh stir-fry vegetable mix

3 eggs, beaten lightly

2 cloves garlic, crushed

4 green onions (scallions), sliced thinly diagonally

⅔ cup (100g) roasted unsalted peanuts, chopped coarsely

⅓ cup (25g) fried asian shallots

150g (4½ ounces) bean sprouts

½ cup loosely packed coriander (cilantro) leaves

1 lime, halved

1 Place noodles in a large heatproof bowl; cover with boiling water. Stand 15 minutes or until just tender. Drain noodles, toss with 2 teaspoons of the oil; cover with plastic wrap to prevent drying out.

2 Stir the boiling water, sugar, tamarind, juice and tamari in a small jug or bowl until sugar dissolves.

3 Heat a wok over high heat; add 1 tablespoon of the oil. Add vegetable mix; stir-fry for 2 minutes or until vegetables are tender; remove from wok.

4 Add egg to wok; swirl to coat base and side. Cook egg for 1 minute or until just set. Transfer to a board; coarsely chop.

5 Heat remaining oil and the garlic in wok; stir-fry for 1 minute or until garlic is fragrant. Return vegetables to wok with noodles, three-quarters of the green onion and sauce mixture; stir-fry until noodles are heated through. Stir in chopped egg.

6 Remove from heat. Sprinkle over half the peanuts and half the shallots; toss to combine.

7 Serve noodles topped with bean sprouts, coriander and remaining peanuts, green onion and shallots; serve pad thai with lime halves.

Meat
FREE

Gluten
FREE

Honey-lemon
PRAWN STIR-FRY

PREP & COOKING TIME 25 MINUTES SERVES 4

1 teaspoon sesame seeds

2 tablespoons vegetable oil

1kg (2 pounds) medium uncooked king prawns (shrimp), shelled, deveined, tails intact

1 large brown onion (200g), cut into thin wedges

½ medium wombok (napa cabbage) (500g), chopped coarsely

1 large carrot (180g), cut into matchsticks

⅓ cup (80ml) lemon juice

2 tablespoons honey

20g (¾-ounce) piece fresh ginger, cut into matchsticks

450g (14½ ounces) packaged microwave jasmine rice

4 green onions (scallions), sliced thinly

¼ cup loosely packed fresh coriander (cilantro) leaves

1 Toast sesame seeds in a heated wok until browned lightly; remove from wok.
2 Heat half the oil in wok over high heat; stir-fry prawns for 2 minutes or until prawns change colour. Remove from wok.
3 Heat remaining oil in wok over medium-high heat; stir-fry brown onion for 3 minutes or until tender. Return prawns to wok with wombok, carrot, juice, honey and ginger; stir-fry until hot. Season to taste.
4 Meanwhile, heat rice according to packet directions.
5 Serve stir-fry with rice, sprinkled with sesame seeds, green onions and coriander.

tips To save time, buy already shelled and deveined prawns from your fishmonger; you will need 500g (1 pound). Have everything prepared before you start to cook. Use brown rice instead of jasmine, if you like.

'Zucchetti' & MEATBALLS

Cheap
EAT

1

2

3

4

SPAGHETTI-LIKE STRANDS ARE CREATED FROM ZUCCHINI IN THIS RECIPE AND USED INSTEAD OF ACTUAL PASTA, MAKING IT A GREAT GLUTEN-FREE OPTION.

'ZUCCHETTI' & meatballs

PREP & COOK TIME 40 MINUTES **SERVES** 4

- **750g (1½ pounds) gluten-free beef sausages**
- **2 cloves garlic, crushed**
- **450g (14½ ounces) mixed baby heirloom tomatoes, halved if large**
- **2 cups (560g) bottled passata**
- **¼ cup coarsely chopped fresh basil**
- **6 medium zucchini (900g)**
- **½ cup (40g) finely grated parmesan**

1 Squeeze meat from sausages. Add garlic; mix to combine. Roll mixture into balls.

2 Cook meatballs in an oiled large frying pan, over medium-high heat, about 3 minutes or until browned all over. Add tomatoes, passata and half the basil; bring to the boil. Reduce heat; simmer, uncovered, for 5 minutes or until meatballs are cooked through. Season to taste.

3 Meanwhile, using a julienne peeler or spiraliser (see tips), cut zucchini into 'spaghetti'.

4 Add zucchini and half the parmesan to sauce mixture; stir gently. Serve sprinkled with remaining basil and parmesan.

tips Use flavoured sausages instead of plain. If you prefer, cook the sausages whole then slice and add to the tomato mixture. To create the long pasta-like strands of zucchini, you will need a few special tools: a julienne peeler, which looks like a wide bladed vegetable peeler with a serrated rather than a straight blade. You could also use a spiraliser, a hand cranked machine designed to cut vegetables into noodles or ribbons. Both items are available from kitchenware shops.

STICKY APRICOT CHICKEN
with rainbow rice

PREP & COOK TIME 40 MINUTES **SERVES** 4

1kg (2 pounds) chicken wing nibbles (see tips)

⅓ cup (110g) apricot jam

1 teaspoon sweet paprika

2 tablespoons lemon juice

1 tablespoon olive oil

rainbow rice

450g (14½ ounces) packaged microwave basmati rice

2 tablespoons olive oil

2 teaspoons dijon mustard

2 tablespoons lemon juice

300g (9½ ounces) canned corn kernels, drained, rinsed

1 medium red capsicum (bell pepper) (200g), chopped finely

⅓ cup (55g) drained sliced kalamata olives

2 green onions (scallions), sliced thinly

1 Preheat oven to 200°C/400°F.
2 Combine chicken with jam, paprika, juice and oil in a large bowl.
3 Place undrained chicken, in single layer, in a large baking dish. Roast for 30 minutes or until cooked through.
4 Meanwhile, make rainbow rice.
5 Serve chicken with rainbow rice.
rainbow rice Heat rice according to packet directions. Whisk oil, mustard and juice in a large bowl. Gently mix in rice and remaining ingredients; season to taste.

tips Chicken wing nibbles, also sold as drumettes, are chicken wings that have been cut into smaller pieces at the joints; if you can't find them you can use chicken wings (cooking time will increase to about 35 minutes) or you can buy chicken wings and cut them into nibbles yourself, discarding the tips. The chicken and rice is yummy hot or cold, so leftovers would make a great lunch or packed picnic. The wings are sticky, so make sure you have a good supply of paper napkins for sticky fingers.

Dairy
FREE

Healthy
CHOICE

CRISPY FISH
with buckwheat salad

PREP & COOK TIME 30 MINUTES **SERVES** 4

2 tablespoons peanut oil

¼ cup (45g) rice flour

4 x 200g (6½-ounce) firm white fish fillets, skin on

buckwheat salad

100g (3 ounces) snow peas, trimmed

1 tablespoon peanut oil

1 tablespoon light soy sauce

1 teaspoon finely grated fresh ginger

2 tablespoons lime juice

2 teaspoons light brown sugar

1 medium carrot (120g), cut into long matchsticks

1 cup (80g) bean sprouts, trimmed

⅓ cup (65g) roasted buckwheat kernels (see tip)

1 cup loosely packed fresh coriander (cilantro) leaves

1 Make buckwheat salad.
2 Heat oil in a large frying pan over medium heat. Place flour in a shallow bowl; season. Coat fish in flour; shake off excess. Cook fish, skin-side down, for 5 minutes or until golden and crisp; turn fish, cook for 5 minutes or until just cooked through.
3 Serve fish with salad.
buckwheat salad Boil, steam or microwave snow peas until tender; drain. Rinse under cold water; drain. Place peanut oil, sauce, ginger, juice and sugar in a large bowl; whisk well. Add snow peas and remaining ingredients; toss gently. Season to taste.

tip If you can't find roasted buckwheat kernels, roast the kernels in the oven at 180°C/350°F for about 5 minutes; cool before using.

SALT & PEPPER CALAMARI
with lemon aïoli

PREP & COOK TIME 30 MINUTES **SERVES** 4

- **⅓ cup (50g) plain (all-purpose) flour**
- **1½ teaspoons sea salt flakes**
- **1½ teaspoons cracked black pepper**
- **vegetable oil, for deep-frying**
- **2kg (4 pounds) baby calamari, cleaned, hoods sliced into rings**
- **80g (2½ ounces) baby rocket (arugula) leaves**
- **1 small red onion (100g), sliced thinly**
- **250g (8 ounces) baby lebanese cucumbers (qukes), sliced thinly lengthways (see tips)**
- **1 medium lemon (140g), halved**

lemon aïoli

- **1½ cups (450g) whole-egg mayonnaise**
- **2 teaspoons finely grated lemon rind**
- **2 tablespoons lemon juice**
- **1 clove garlic, crushed**

1 Make lemon aïoli.
2 Combine flour, salt and pepper in a large bowl.
3 Fill a large wok one-third full with oil; heat to 180°C/350°F (or until a cube of bread turns golden in 10 seconds). Working in batches, toss calamari in flour mixture; shake away excess. Fry calamari for 2 minutes or until golden and just tender; drain on paper towel.
4 Combine rocket, onion and cucumber in a large bowl. Serve calamari with rocket salad, aïoli and lemon halves.
lemon aïoli Combine ingredients in a small bowl.

tips Use a vegetable peeler to slice the cucumbers lengthways into long thin ribbons. For a gluten-free option you could use gluten-free plain flour.

Gluten
FREE

LAMB CHOPS
with peach caprese salad

PREP & COOK TIME 25 MINUTES **SERVES** 4

8 lamb loin chops (800g)

1½ tablespoons extra virgin olive oil

4 medium peaches (600g), sliced thickly

250g (8 ounces) buffalo mozzarella, torn

400g (12½ ounces) baby heirloom tomatoes, halved

½ cup loosely packed fresh small basil leaves

1 tablespoon white wine vinegar

pistachio mint pesto

½ cup (70g) pistachios

1½ cups loosely packed fresh mint leaves

1 cup loosely packed fresh flat-leaf parsley leaves

1 clove garlic, crushed

2 teaspoons finely grated lemon rind

2 teaspoons lemon juice

½ cup (125ml) extra virgin olive oil

1 Make pistachio mint pesto.

2 Combine lamb and 1 tablespoon of the oil in a medium bowl; season. Cook lamb on a lightly oiled heated grill plate (or grill or barbecue) for about 3 minutes each side, adding peaches to the grill plate for the last 2 minutes of lamb cooking time or until lamb is cooked as desired and peaches are golden.

3 Layer peaches with mozzarella, tomato and basil; drizzle with combined vinegar and remaining oil. Serve salad with lamb and pesto.

pistachio mint pesto Blend or process ingredients until smooth; season to taste.

tips Buffalo mozzarella has a tangier flavour than cow's milk mozzarella which may be substituted for it. You could use figs, apple or pear instead of peaches, if they are unavailable. For a nut-free pesto you could use pepitas (pumpkin seed kernels) instead of the pistachios.

SESAME-CRUSTED CHICKEN
with 'quickled' slaw

PREP & COOK TIME 25 MINUTES (PLUS STANDING) **SERVES** 4

⅔ cup (100g) plain (all-purpose) flour

2 eggs

1 cup (75g) panko (japanese) breadcrumbs

¼ cup (40g) white sesame seeds

¼ cup (50g) black sesame seeds

12 chicken tenderloins (900g)

vegetable oil, for shallow-frying

1 lime, halved

micro herbs, to serve (optional)

'quickled' slaw

1 lebanese cucumber (130g)

400g (12½ ounces) baby carrots (dutch carrots), trimmed

¼ small red cabbage (300g)

½ cup (125ml) white wine vinegar

1 tablespoon caster (superfine) sugar

½ teaspoon sea salt flakes

lime mayonnaise

1 cup (300g) japanese mayonnaise

2 teaspoons finely grated lime rind

1 tablespoon lime juice

1 Make 'quickled' slaw. Make lime mayonnaise.

2 Place flour in a shallow bowl; season. In another shallow bowl, lightly beat eggs. Place breadcrumbs and sesame seeds in a third shallow bowl; toss to combine. Coat chicken tenderloins in flour, dip in egg, allow excess to drip off, then coat in breadcrumb mixture.

3 Heat 1cm (½-inch) oil in a large frying pan over medium heat. Cook chicken, in batches, turning frequently, for 3½ minutes or until golden and cooked through. Remove with a slotted spoon; drain on paper towel.

4 Serve chicken with slaw, mayonnaise and lime halves, sprinkled with micro herbs, if you like.

'quickled' slaw Using a vegetable peeler, mandoline or V-slicer, cut cucumber and carrots lengthways into long thin ribbons. Finely shred cabbage. Combine vegetables with remaining ingredients in a large glass or ceramic (non-reactive bowl); stand 15 minutes. Drain.

lime mayonnaise Combine ingredients in a small bowl; season to taste.

Dairy
FREE

MUSTARD CHICKEN
with potato & corn smash

PREP & COOK TIME 30 MINUTES SERVES 4

- **1kg (2 pounds) baby new (chat) potatoes**
- **4 x 200g (6½-ounce) chicken breast fillets**
- **cooking-oil spray**
- **1 tablespoon wholegrain mustard**
- **400g (12½ ounces) canned corn kernels, drained, rinsed**
- **⅓ cup (80g) sour cream**
- **¼ cup finely chopped fresh chives**
- **60g (2 ounces) mixed baby salad leaves**
- **1 lebanese cucumber (130g), sliced into long thin ribbons**
- **2 tablespoons lemon juice**
- **1 tablespoon extra virgin olive oil**
- **1 medium lemon (140g), cut into wedges**

1 Boil, steam or microwave potato until tender; drain.

2 Meanwhile, spray chicken with cooking oil; cook chicken on a heated grill plate (or grill or barbecue), over medium heat, brushing occasionally with mustard, about 5 minutes each side or until cooked through. Cover chicken; stand 5 minutes, then slice thickly.

3 Combine potato, corn, sour cream and chives in a large bowl; use a potato masher or back of a fork to crush mixture. Season to taste.

4 Place salad leaves, cucumber, lemon juice and olive oil in a large bowl; toss gently.

5 Serve chicken with potato smash, salad and lemon wedges.

tip Use a vegetable peeler to slice the cucumber lengthways into long thin ribbons.

PORK FILET MIGNON
with mushroom sauce

PREP & COOK TIME 30 MINUTES **SERVES** 4

16 fresh sage leaves

4 slices prosciutto (260g)

4 x 250g (8-ounce) pork fillets

2 tablespoons olive oil

200g (6½ ounces) thinly sliced swiss brown mushrooms

1 small brown onion (80g), sliced thinly

1 clove garlic, crushed

1½ cups (375ml) beef stock

1 tablespoon tomato paste

125g (4 ounces) frozen chopped spinach

475g (15-ounce) tub cheesy mashed potato

1 Place two sage leaves along each slice of prosciutto. Wrap one slice of prosciutto around each pork fillet; secure with toothpicks.

2 Cook pork on a heated oiled grill plate (or grill or barbecue), over medium-high heat, turning, for 10 minutes or until browned all over and cooked as desired. Remove from pan; cover to keep warm.

3 Meanwhile, heat oil in a medium frying pan on high heat. Cook the remaining sage leaves for 30 seconds or until crisp. Remove from pan with a slotted spoon; drain on paper towel. Reduce heat to medium-high. Cook mushrooms, onion and garlic in same pan, stirring occasionally, for 4 minutes or until mushrooms are golden and tender. Add stock and paste; bring to the boil, Reduce heat; simmer, for 5 minutes or until sauce thickens slightly.

4 Meanwhile, microwave spinach on HIGH (100%) about 1 minute or until hot. Place spinach in a fine sieve; squeeze out excess water. Heat mash according to packet directions. Transfer to a large bowl; stir spinach into mash; season.

5 Serve thickly sliced pork with mash and mushroom sauce; sprinkle with crisp sage leaves.

Dairy
FREE

PRAWN CLUB SANDWICHES
with baked chips

PREP & COOK TIME 35 MINUTES **SERVES** 4

800g (1½ pounds) frozen potato chips

2 teaspoons olive oil

4 streaky bacon rashers (100g), each cut into three even pieces

½ cup (150g) whole-egg mayonnaise

2 teaspoons tomato sauce (ketchup)

few drops of Tabasco

8 slices white sourdough bread (560g)

1 small green oak leaf lettuce, leaves separated

2 medium tomatoes (300g), sliced thinly

500g (1 pound) shelled cooked tiger prawns (shrimp)

1 Preheat oven to 220°C/425°F.

2 Place chips on a baking-paper-lined oven tray, season; cook in oven, according to packet directions.

3 Meanwhile, heat oil in a large frying pan over high heat; cook bacon for 5 minutes or until crisp. Drain on paper towel.

4 Combine mayonnaise, ketchup and tabasco to taste in a small bowl. Spread bread with mayonnaise mixture. Sandwich lettuce, bacon, tomato and prawns between bread slices. Serve with chips.

Beetroot, blood orange & PORK SALAD

PREP & COOK TIME 40 MINUTES **SERVES** 4

- 500g (1 pound) pork fillet, trimmed
- 1 wholemeal baguette (240g), halved horizontally, halved crossways
- 2 tablespoons olive oil
- 450g (14½ ounces) canned baby beetroots (beets), drained, halved
- 3 small blood oranges (570g), peeled, sliced thinly
- 150g (4½ ounces) mixed baby salad leaves
- 8 fresh dates (160g), halved, seeded
- ½ cup (60g) seeded kalamata olives
- 2 tablespoons pepitas (pumpkin seed kernels), roasted
- 2 tablespoons sunflower seeds, roasted
- 2 teaspoons poppy seeds

raspberry dressing

- 2 tablespoons raspberry wine vinegar
- 2 tablespoons olive oil
- 1 small clove garlic, crushed
- 2 teaspoons finely chopped fresh chives

1 Make raspberry dressing.

2 Drizzle pork and bread with oil; season. Cook pork on a lightly oiled heated grill plate (or grill or barbecue), turning frequently, for 15 minutes or until cooked through. Rest for 5 minutes before slicing thickly. Place bread on the oiled heated grill plate for 2 minutes each side or until golden. Tear bread into large pieces.

3 Place pork in a large bowl with beetroot, blood oranges, salad leaves, dates, olives and dressing; toss to combine. Sprinkle salad with seeds, serve with bread.

raspberry dressing Combine ingredients in a small bowl; season to taste.

tips You can use navel oranges if blood oranges are not available. You can use grilled haloumi, lamb fillets or chicken breast or thigh fillets instead of the pork, if you like.

Healthy
CHOICE

Gluten
FREE

VEAL WITH
lemon & capers

PREP & COOK TIME 35 MINUTES **SERVES** 6

- **2 cups (500ml) water**
- **1 cup (170g) polenta**
- **¾ cup (180ml) skim milk**
- **¼ cup (20g) finely grated parmesan**
- **1 tablespoon cracked black pepper**
- **6 thin veal schnitzels (600g) (see tips)**
- **60g (2 ounces) butter**
- **1 tablespoon drained baby capers, rinsed**
- **3 strips lemon rind, sliced thinly**
- **⅓ cup (80ml) lemon juice**
- **¼ cup micro parsley**

1 Bring the water to the boil in a medium saucepan. Stir in polenta, reduce heat to low; cook, stirring, for 10 minutes or until polenta thickens. Stir in milk; cook, stirring, for 5 minutes or until polenta thickens. Stir in parmesan; season to taste.

2 Meanwhile, sprinkle pepper on both sides of veal. Heat butter in a large frying pan over medium-high heat; cook steaks, in batches, until browned lightly both sides. Remove veal from pan; cover to keep warm.

3 Add capers, rind, juice and 1 tablespoon water to pan; bring to the boil, stirring. Spoon sauce over veal; sprinkle with parsley. Serve polenta with veal.

serving suggestion Serve veal with steamed green beans and sprinkle polenta with extra grated parmesan, if you prefer.

tips Veal schnitzel is thinly sliced steak available crumbed or plain (uncrumbed); we used plain schnitzel, also called escalopes in this recipe. You could serve the veal with mashed potato instead of polenta, if you prefer.

Thai chicken OMELETTES

PREP & COOK TIME 30 MINUTES SERVES 4

2 tablespoons peanut oil

400g (14½ ounces) chicken breast fillets, sliced thinly

1 small brown onion (80g), sliced thinly

2 cloves garlic, crushed

2 tablespoons oyster sauce

8 eggs

1 teaspoon fish sauce

1 teaspoon soy sauce

100g (3 ounces) enoki mushrooms

½ cup loosely packed fresh mint

½ cup loosely packed fresh thai basil leaves

1 cup (80g) bean sprouts

2 limes, cut into wedges

1 Heat 2 teaspoons of the oil in a wok over high heat; stir-fry chicken, in batches, until browned. Remove from wok.

2 Heat another 2 teaspoons of the oil in wok; stir-fry onion and garlic until fragrant. Return chicken to wok with oyster sauce; stir-fry until hot. Remove from wok; cover to keep warm.

3 Whisk eggs with fish and soy sauces in a large jug. Heat 1 teaspoon of the oil in same wok. Place the egg mixture in a plastic ziptop bag. Snip a small hole in one corner and drizzle ¼ cup of the mixture into a heated wok; cook until almost set. Transfer omelette onto a serving plate; cover to keep warm. Repeat to make a total of eight omelettes.

4 Fill omelettes with chicken mixture, mushrooms, herbs and sprouts. Serve with lime.

tips Enoki mushrooms have clumps of long, spaghetti-like stems with tiny, snowy white caps. They are available from Asian food shops and supermarkets. You can use coriander (cilantro) if thai basil is unavailable. If you like it spicy you can add some sliced red chilli to your chicken omelettes before serving.

Dairy FREE

CRUMBED LAMB CUTLETS
with orange & couscous salad

PREP & COOK TIME 40 MINUTES **SERVES** 4

¼ cup (35g) plain (all-purpose) flour

1 egg

⅔ cup (50g) stale breadcrumbs

2 tablespoons za'atar (see tip)

2 teaspoons chopped fresh thyme

12 french-trimmed lamb cutlets (600g)

vegetable oil, for shallow-frying

½ cup (100g) couscous

½ cup (125ml) boiling water

2 medium oranges (480g), peeled, sliced

1 cup (120g) pitted kalamata olives

100g (3 ounces) fetta, crumbled

125g (4 ounces) baby spinach leaves

1 small red onion (100g), cut into thin wedges

⅓ cup (80ml) olive oil

2 tablespoons white wine vinegar

1 Place flour in a shallow bowl; season. In another shallow bowl, lightly beat egg. Combine breadcrumbs, za'atar and thyme in a third shallow bowl. Coat cutlets in flour, dip in egg, allow excess to drip off, then coat in breadcrumb mixture.
2 Heat 1cm (½-inch) oil in a large frying pan over medium heat. Cook cutlets, in batches, for 2 minutes each side or until golden and cooked through. Remove with a slotted spoon; drain on paper towel.
3 Meanwhile, combine couscous with the boiling water in a large heatproof bowl, cover; stand about 5 minutes or until water is absorbed, fluffing with fork occasionally. Add remaining ingredients; mix well.
4 Serve cutlets with orange and couscous salad.

tip Za'atar is a blend of roasted dry herbs, spices, sesame seeds and salt and is available from Middle-Eastern food shops and some delicatessens. To make your own, combine 1 tablespoon each sumac and sesame seeds with 2 teaspoons finely chopped fresh thyme and 1 teaspoon salt.

MONGOLIAN BEEF *with noodles*

PREP & COOK TIME 25 MINUTES **SERVES** 4

600g (1¼ pounds) beef eye fillet, sliced thinly

⅓ cup (80ml) sweet sherry

2 tablespoons dark soy sauce

2 tablespoons sweet chilli sauce

2 tablespoons vegetable oil

1 large brown onion (200g), sliced thinly

2 cloves garlic, crushed

1 medium red capsicum (bell pepper) (200g), sliced thinly

235g (7½ ounces) choy sum, cut into 10cm (4-inch) lengths

1 tablespoon brown sugar

1 teaspoon sesame oil

⅓ cup (80ml) chicken stock

400g (12½ ounces) thick hokkien noodles

1 Combine beef with half the sherry, half the soy sauce and half the sweet chilli sauce in a medium bowl.

2 Heat half the vegetable oil in a wok over high heat; stir-fry beef, in batches, for 2 minutes or until browned. Remove from wok.

3 Heat remaining vegetable oil in wok; stir-fry onion and garlic, for 3 minutes or until onion softens. Add capsicum and choy sum; stir-fry until vegetables are tender.

4 Return beef to wok with remaining ingredients; stir-fry until hot.

tip Broccolini or gai lan would work well instead of choy sum in this stir-fry.

Dairy
FREE

Healthy
CHOICE

Rosemary TURKEY SKEWERS

PREP & COOK TIME 35 MINUTES **SERVES** 4

8 sprigs fresh rosemary

600g (1¼ pounds) minced (ground) turkey

1 egg

2 cloves garlic, crushed

1 tablespoon tomato paste

1 cup (70g) stale breadcrumbs

2 tablespoons olive oil

1 large brown onion (200g), sliced thinly

1 tablespoon plain (all-purpose) flour

1 cup (250ml) beef stock

2 medium tomatoes (300g), chopped coarsely

450g (14½ ounces) packaged white microwave rice

200g (6½ ounces) green beans, trimmed

1 Remove two-thirds of the leaves from the bottom part of each rosemary sprig to make skewers. Finely chop 2 teaspoons of the leaves and reserve.

2 Combine turkey, egg, garlic, paste, breadcrumbs and reserved chopped rosemary in a medium bowl. Shape turkey mixture into sausage shapes on rosemary skewers.

3 Cook skewers on a heated oiled grill plate (or grill or barbecue) over medium-high heat, turning, for 10 minutes or until browned and cooked through. Remove from pan; cover to keep warm.

4 Heat oil in a large frying pan over medium heat; cook onion, stirring, until soft. Add flour; cook, stirring, until mixture bubbles and thickens. Gradually stir in stock until smooth. Add tomato; cook, stirring, until gravy boils and thickens.

5 Meanwhile, heat rice according to packet directions. Microwave beans on HIGH (100%) about 1 minute or until tender.

6 Serve skewers with gravy, rice and beans.

Sweet chilli chicken & BLAT SALAD

PREP & COOK TIME 25 MINUTES **SERVES** 4

4 chicken breast fillets (800g)

2 tablespoons olive oil

½ cup (125ml) sweet chilli sauce

1 clove garlic, crushed

⅓ cup (80ml) lime juice

8 streaky bacon slices (200g)

250g (8 ounces) cherry truss tomatoes

⅓ cup (100g) mayonnaise

1 tablespoon finely chopped fresh flat-leaf parsley

2 baby cos (romaine) lettuce, leaves separated

1 medium avocado (250g), sliced thinly lengthways

1 Heat an oiled grill plate (or grill pan or barbecue) over medium heat.

2 Combine chicken, oil, sauce, garlic and half the juice in a medium bowl; season. Cook chicken, in batches, on grill, for 5 minutes each side or until cooked. Remove from heat, cover to keep warm.

3 Meanwhile, cook bacon and tomatoes on grill over medium heat until bacon is crisp and tomatoes begin to soften.

4 Combine mayonnaise, remaining juice and parsley in a small bowl.

5 Arrange lettuce on serving plates; top with chicken, bacon, tomatoes and avocado; drizzle with dressing.

serving suggestion Serve with sourdough bread and lime cheeks.

Gluten
FREE

LEMON GRASS & LIME PRAWNS
with broccoli rice

PREP & COOK TIME 15 MINUTES **SERVES** 4

500g (1 pound) broccoli, chopped finely

80g (2 ounces) butter

10cm (4-inch) stick fresh lemon grass (20g), chopped finely

500g (1 pound) shelled uncooked medium king prawns (shrimp)

1 tablespoon finely grated lime rind

2 tablespoons lime juice

2 tablespoons finely chopped fresh coriander (cilantro)

2 green onions (scallions), sliced thinly

2 limes, halved

1 Process broccoli, in batches, until finely chopped and resembles rice grains. Blanch in a medium saucepan of boiling water for 20 seconds; drain. Spread on paper towel to dry; season to taste. Cover to keep warm.

2 Melt butter in a large frying pan over medium heat; cook, lemon grass, stirring, for 1 minute or until fragrant. Increase heat to high, add prawns and half the rind. Cook, stirring, until prawns change colour. Remove from heat; stir in juice and coriander.

3 Top broccoli rice with prawn mixture, remaining rind and the green onion. Serve with lime halves.

Cheat's roast LAMB DINNER

PREP & COOK TIME 30 MINUTES **SERVES** 4

- **8 thick lamb sausages (1.2kg)**
- **800g (1½ pounds) potatoes, chopped coarsely**
- **500g (1 pound) frozen broad beans (fava beans)**
- **400g (12½ ounces) baby carrots (dutch carrots), trimmed**
- **40g (1½ ounces) butter**
- **½ cup (125ml) hot milk**
- **¼ cup loosely packed small fresh mint leaves**

mint sauce

- **2 cups firmly packed fresh mint leaves**
- **2 cloves garlic, quartered**
- **½ cup (125ml) olive oil**
- **¼ cup (60ml) white wine vinegar**
- **1 tablespoon caster sugar**

1 Cook sausages on a heated grill plate (or grill or barbecue), turning, about 8 minutes or until cooked through.

2 Meanwhile, boil, steam or microwave potato, beans and carrots, separately, until tender; drain. Cover carrots to keep warm. Push potato through a fine sieve into large bowl; stir in butter and milk until smooth. Peel broad beans. Place beans in a small bowl; crush coarsely with fork. Fold beans into potato mixture. Season to taste; cover to keep warm.

3 Make mint sauce.

4 Serve sausages with mint sauce, carrots and broad bean mash; sprinkle with mint leaves. Season.

mint sauce Blend or process mint and garlic until smooth; with motor operating, gradually add oil, in a thin steady stream, until mixture is smooth. Stir in vinegar and sugar.

tip Broad beans are available both frozen and fresh from most supermarkets. If you can't find any, you can use frozen peas in the mash, instead.

Cheap
EAT

FAST PASTA

Mediterranean MAC & CHEESE

PREP & COOK TIME 35 MINUTES
SERVES 4

Cook 375g (12oz) elbow macaroni in a large saucepan of boiling salted water until tender; drain. Meanwhile, melt 60g (2oz) butter in a large saucepan over medium heat, add ⅓ cup plain (all-purpose) flour; cook, stirring, for 2 minutes or until mixture bubbles and thickens. Gradually stir in 3 cups milk. Add ⅓ cup tomato paste; cook, stirring, until sauce boils and thickens. Preheat grill (broiler). Stir pasta, a drained 320g (10oz) jar antipasto mixed vegetables, ⅓ cup finely chopped fresh chives and ¾ cup pizza cheese into sauce. Place mixture in deep 2-litre (8-cup) ovenproof dish; sprinkle with another ¾ cup pizza cheese. Grill until cheese melts and is browned lightly.

Pumpkin, spinach & RICOTTA AGNOLOTTI

PREP & COOK TIME 25 MINUTES
SERVES 4

Cook 625g (1¼lbs) fresh ricotta and spinach agnolotti in a large saucepan of boiling salted water until cooked through; drain. Melt 50g (1½oz) butter in same cleaned pan over medium heat; cook 1 bunch trimmed and finely shredded spinach with 1 teaspoon ground cinnamon until wilted. Remove from pan. Add 1kg (2lbs) canned pumpkin soup to pan, bring to the boil; boil for 2 minutes. Add ½ cup pouring cream, spinach and agnolotti; stirring until well combined and heated through. Remove from heat. Stand 5 minutes before serving. Season to taste. Serve agnolotti, topped with 100g (3oz) crumbled fresh ricotta and fresh flat-leaf parsley leaves.

tip We used agnolotti, a half-moon shaped filled pasta but you can use any vegetarian-style filled pasta you prefer.

Turkey BOLOGNESE

PREP & COOK TIME 30 MINUTES
SERVES 4

Cook 375g (12oz) fettuccine in a large saucepan of boiling salted water until just tender; drain. Meanwhile, heat 1 tablespoon olive oil in a large frying pan over high heat; cook 1 finely chopped medium brown onion and 2 crushed garlic cloves, stirring, for 3 minutes or until onion softens. Add 1 finely chopped medium carrot and 1 finely chopped stick celery; cook, stirring, for 5 minutes or until vegetables are just tender. Add 500g (1lb) minced (ground) turkey; cook, stirring, until turkey is changed in colour. Add 2 cups passata and ½ cup chicken stock; bring to the boil. Reduce heat; simmer, uncovered, for 15 minutes or until the mixture thickens slightly. Add ½ cup frozen peas; cook, stirring, until heated through. Season to taste. Serve pasta topped with bolognese sauce and ⅓ cup shaved parmesan.

Chicken pesto pasta WITH TOMATOES

PREP & COOK TIME 25 MINUTES
SERVES 4

Preheat grill (broiler). Place 250g (8oz) cherry truss tomatoes with stems attached on an oven tray. Drizzle with 1 teaspoon balsamic glaze; grill about 10 minutes or until tomato skins begin to split. Meanwhile, cook 375g (12oz) penne pasta in a large saucepan of boiling salted water until tender; drain, reserving ⅓ cup of the cooking liquid. Return pasta to pan with ⅓ cup basil pesto, 2 cups shredded barbecued chicken, tomatoes and reserved cooking liquid. Stir gently over low heat until heated through. Serve sprinkled with 2 tablespoons finely grated parmesan and some micro basil.

Cheap
EAT

Butter chicken HAND PIES

PREP & COOK TIME 40 MINUTES MAKES 4

20g (¾ ounce) butter

1 small brown onion (80g), chopped finely

250g (8 ounces) minced (ground) chicken

1 small carrot (70g), grated coarsely

2 tablespoons butter chicken curry paste

2 tablespoons frozen peas

2 sheets puff pastry

1 egg, beaten lightly

⅓ cup loosely packed fresh small mint leaves

80g (2½ ounces) baby rocket (arugula) leaves

minty yoghurt

½ cup (140g) greek-style yoghurt

2 tablespoons finely chopped freah mint leaves

1 Preheat oven to 220°C/425°F. Line oven tray with baking paper.

2 Melt butter in a large frying pan over medium-high heat; cook onion, stirring, about 3 minutes or until soft. Add chicken; cook, stirring, until browned. Add carrot, paste and peas; cook for 5 minutes or until thickened. Season to taste.

3 Cut each pastry sheet into quarters (you will have eight squares). Place four pastry squares on trays; divide mixture evenly into the centre of pastry squares. Brush edges with egg.

4 Gently fold remaining pastry squares in half; using kitchen scissors cut 3 slits in the centre of each triangle. Open pastry squares out; place over chicken filling. Press pastry edges together to seal; brush with egg.

5 Bake about 25 minutes or until browned.

6 Meanwhile, make minty yoghurt.

7 Serve pies with mint leaves, rocket and minty yoghurt.

minty yoghurt Combine ingredients in a small bowl.

Corn & quinoa CHOWDER

PREP & COOK TIME 40 MINUTES (PLUS STANDING) **SERVES** 4

2 tablespoons olive oil

4 corn cobs (1.6kg), trimmed, kernels removed

1 large brown onion (200g), chopped finely

1 large potato (300g), peeled, chopped coarsely

2 cloves garlic, crushed

1 teaspoon smoked paprika

1 litre (4 cups) vegetable stock

½ cup (125ml) pouring cream

⅓ cup (70g) red or white quinoa

¾ cup (180ml) water

⅓ cup loosely packed fresh coriander (cilantro) leaves

4 x 21cm (8½-inch) wholegrain tortillas, toasted, torn

2 limes (130g), halved

guacamole

1 medium avocado (250g), mashed coarsely

1 green onion (scallion), sliced thinly

2 tablespoons lime juice

1 Heat oil in a large saucepan over medium heat; cook corn, onion and potato, covered, for 10 minutes or until onion softens. Add garlic and half of the paprika; cook, stirring, for 1 minute or until fragrant.

2 Add stock and cream; bring to the boil over high heat. Reduce heat to medium; cook, covered, for 10 minutes or until potato is tender. Remove from heat; stand 10 minutes. Blend or process half the chowder until almost smooth; return to pan. Season to taste. Stir over heat until hot.

3 Meanwhile, place quinoa and the water in a small saucepan; bring to the boil. Reduce heat to low; cook, covered, for 12 minutes or until tender. Stand, covered, for 10 minutes; fluff with a fork. Stir quinoa through chowder.

4 Make guacamole.

5 Ladle chowder into bowls; top with guacamole, coriander and remaining paprika. Serve with tortillas and lime.

guacamole Combine avocado, green onion and juice in a small bowl; season to taste.

tip If using a jug blender or food processor to blend soup, make sure it is cool before blending. The heat build-up can cause the lid to blow off.

Meat
FREE

HOKKIEN MEE *with lamb*

PREP & COOK TIME 20 MINUTES **SERVES** 4

300g (9½ ounces) thin hokkien noodles

1 tablespoon vegetable oil

700g (1½ pounds) lamb strips

1 medium brown onion (150g), sliced thinly

2 teaspoons finely grated fresh ginger

2 cloves garlic, crushed

200g (6½ ounces) sugar snap peas, trimmed, halved lengthways

1 medium yellow capsicum (bell pepper) (200g), sliced thinly

1 medium zucchini (120g), cut into ribbons

2 cups finely shredded wombok (napa cabbage)

⅓ cup (80ml) hoisin sauce

1 tablespoon dark soy sauce

1 tablespoon hot water

⅓ cup loosely packed small fresh mint leaves

1 Place noodles in a medium heatproof bowl, cover with boiling water; separate with a fork, drain.

2 Heat half the oil in a wok over high heat; stir-fry lamb, in batches, until browned. Remove from wok.

3 Heat remaining oil in wok; stir-fry onion for 2 minutes or until soft. Add ginger and garlic; stir-fry 30 seconds or until fragrant. Add snap peas, capsicum, zucchini and wombok; stir-fry until tender.

4 Return lamb to wok with noodles, sauces and the hot water; stir-fry until heated through. Serve sprinkled with mint.

tips You can use 400g (12½ ounces) packaged fresh stir-fry vegetables instead of the peas, capsicum, zucchini, wombok. Dark soy sauce is deep brown, almost black in colour; it is rich, with a thicker consistency than other types. Pungent but not particularly salty, it is good for marinating. Available from Asian supermarkets.

Chicken, asparagus & KALE CEASAR SALAD

PREP & COOK TIME 40 MINUTES **SERVES** 4

12 thin slices sourdough baguette (100g)
¾ cup (60g) finely grated parmesan
1 tablespoon olive oil
8 slices prosciutto (120g)
300g (9½ ounces) asparagus, trimmed, halved lengthways
4 eggs
100g (3 ounces) trimmed kale leaves, torn
400g (12½ ounces) shredded skinless barbecued chicken

green goddess dressing

¼ cup (75g) whole-egg mayonnaise
2 tablespoons sour cream
¼ cup coarsely chopped fresh flat-leaf parsley
1 tablespoon coarsely chopped fresh basil
1 tablespoon coarsely chopped fresh chives
1 tablespoon lemon juice
1 clove garlic, chopped finely

1 Make green goddess dressing.

2 Preheat grill (broiler). Toast bread on one side, then turn and sprinkle with half the parmesan; grill croûtons until parmesan melts and is browned lightly.

3 Heat oil in a small frying pan over medium heat; cook prosciutto until golden and crisp. Remove from pan; drain on paper towel. Cook asparagus in same pan, stirring, for 5 minutes or until browned lightly and tender.

4 Place eggs in a medium saucepan, cover with cold water; stir gently (this centres the yolks) over high heat until water comes to the boil. Boil about 1½ minutes or until soft-boiled. Drain eggs, rinse under cold water. Peel eggs.

5 Meanwhile, place kale and one-quarter of the dressing in a large bowl; toss to combine. Stand for 5 minutes to soften slightly.

6 Add croûtons, chicken, prosciutto, asparagus, remaining parmesan and dressing; toss to combine. Serve salad topped with halved eggs.

green goddess dressing Process ingredients until smooth and combined; season to taste. (Makes ¾ cup)

tip For a meat-free meal omit the chicken and prosciutto; add some more grilled asparagus or swiss brown mushrooms.

Healthy
CHOICE

FIVE-SPICE PORK
with almonds

PREP & COOK TIME 35 MINUTES **SERVES** 4

- **750g (1½ pounds) pork fillets, sliced thinly**
- **1 teaspoon garam masala**
- **2 teaspoons chinese five-spice powder**
- **1 tablespoon peanut oil**
- **1 medium carrot (120g), cut into long thin strips**
- **2 cloves garlic, crushed**
- **1 tablespoon finely grated fresh ginger**
- **4 baby pak choy choy (600g), halved lengthways**
- **1 tablespoon sweet chilli sauce**
- **¼ cup (60ml) oyster sauce**
- **2 tablespoons lime juice**
- **2 tablespoons hot water**
- **100g (3 ounces) snow peas, trimmed**
- **1 cup (80g) bean sprouts**
- **⅓ cup (55g) blanched almonds, roasted, chopped coarsely**
- **1 lime (65g), cut into wedges**

1 Combine pork and spices in a large bowl; mix well.
2 Heat half the oil in a wok over high heat; stir-fry pork mixture, in batches, until pork is browned and tender, remove from wok.
3 Heat remaining oil in wok; add carrot, garlic and ginger. Stir-fry for 2 minutes, then add pak choy, sauces, juice and the hot water; stir-fry for 4 minutes or until pak choy is tender.
4 Return pork to wok with snow peas; stir-fry until heated through. Top with sprouts and nuts. Serve with lime.

serving suggestion Serve with rice noodles or steamed rice.
tips You can substitute the pork with chicken, lamb or beef. For a nut-free version use vegetable oil instead of peanut oil and replace the almonds with fried Asian shallots.

EXPRESS WEEKEND

'FINGER-LICKIN' LAMB RIBS with nashi slaw

PREP & COOK TIME 40 MINUTES **SERVES** 4

2kg (4 pounds) lamb rib racks

400g (12½ ounces) packaged shredded coleslaw mix

1 medium nashi pear (200g), sliced thinly

½ cup (125ml) coleslaw dressing

barbecue sauce

1 cup (250ml) tomato sauce (ketchup)

¾ cup (180ml) apple cider vinegar

2 tablespoons olive oil

¼ cup (60ml) worcestershire sauce

⅓ cup (75g) firmly packed light brown sugar

2 tablespoons american-style mustard

1 teaspoon cracked black pepper

2 cloves garlic, crushed

2 tablespoons lemon juice

1 Make barbecue sauce.

2 Place ribs in a large shallow dish; pour barbecue sauce over ribs; turn to coat in sauce.

3 Drain ribs; reserve sauce. Cook ribs on a heated oiled grill plate (or grill or barbecue), brushing occasionally with reserved sauce, for about 15 minutes or until cooked, turning ribs halfway through cooking time.

4 Bring any remaining sauce to the boil in a small saucepan; boil, uncovered, for about 5 minutes or until sauce thickens slightly.

5 Meanwhile, combine coleslaw, nashi pear and dressing in a medium bowl. Season to taste.

6 Cut ribs into serving-sized pieces; serve with hot barbecue sauce and coleslaw.

barbecue sauce Bring ingredients to the boil in a medium saucepan. Cool for 10 minutes.

tips Because it contains raw meat juices, the barbecue sauce used for marinating must be boiled for the time stated. Use a julienne peeler or a mandoline or V-slicer with a julienne attachment to cut the nashi pear. There are many good barbecue marinades available in supermarkets today; you could use a smoky barbecue sauce marinade instead of the barbecue sauce in this recipe, just add a little vegetable oil, to prevent it sticking to the barbecue or grill plate.

Dairy
FREE

FRAGRANT BEEF CURRY
with crisp coconut topping

PREP & COOK TIME 50 MINUTES **SERVES** 4

2 tablespoons vegetable oil

750g (1½ pounds) beef strips

1 medium brown onion (150g), chopped finely

3 cloves garlic, crushed

10cm (4-inch) stalk fresh lemon grass (20g), chopped finely

1 star anise

1 cinnamon stick

270ml canned coconut cream

1 tablespoon tamarind puree (concentrate)

200g (11 ounces) green beans, trimmed, halved lengthways

1 tablespoon fish sauce

½ cup loosely packed fresh coriander (cilantro) leaves

450g (14½ ounces) packaged jasmine microwave rice

crisp coconut topping

2 tablespoons vegetable oil

4 green onions (scallions), chopped

2 cups (100g) flaked coconut

2 tablespoons light brown sugar

¼ cup (75g) tamarind puree (concentrate)

1 Make crisp coconut topping.

2 Meanwhile, heat half the oil in a wok over high heat; stir-fry beef, in batches, until browned. Remove from wok; cover to keep warm.

3 Heat remaining oil in a wok; stir-fry onion until soft. Add garlic, lemon grass, star anise and cinnamon; stir-fry for 3 minutes or until fragrant. Add coconut cream and tamarind; cook, stirring occasionally, for 5 minutes or until mixture has thickened slightly. Return beef to wok with beans and sauce; stir-fry for 3 minutes or until beans are just tender. Remove from heat; stir in coriander. Remove and discard cinnamon stick before serving.

4 Heat rice according to packet directions. Stir three-quarters of the topping mixture through the rice; scatter remaining topping over curry. Serve curry with rice.

crisp coconut topping Preheat oven to 150°C/300°F. Heat oil in a wok over medium heat; stir-fry remaining ingredients, tossing continuously, for 15 minutes or until browned lightly. Transfer mixture to an oven tray; roast 20 minutes or until mixture has dried.

tip The crisp coconut topping, also known as serundeng, is usually sprinkled over a hot dish just as it's served, much like a gremolata, to awaken the tastebuds.

Moroccan FISH & CHIPS

PREP & COOK TIME 1 HOUR **SERVES** 4

- **¾ cup firmly packed fresh coriander leaves**
- **¼ cup (60ml) olive oil**
- **2 tablespoons lemon juice**
- **6 cloves garlic, quartered**
- **2 teaspoons sweet paprika**
- **½ teaspoon ground cumin**
- **¼ teaspoon cayenne pepper**
- **½ cup (125ml) chicken stock**
- **1kg (2 pounds) kumara (orange sweet potato), cut into thick wedges**
- **1 cup (70g) stale breadcrumbs**
- **2 tablespoons finely chopped fresh flat-leaf parsley**
- **2 teaspoons finely grated lemon rind**
- **4 x 200g (6½-ounce) firm white fish fillets**
- **¼ cup loosely packed fresh coriander (cilantro) leaves, extra**

1 Preheat oven to 200°C/400°F. Oil 2-litre (8-cup) ovenproof dish.

2 Blend or process coriander, 2 tablespoons of the oil, juice, garlic and spices until smooth.

3 Combine spice paste, stock and kumara in prepared dish. Roast 20 minutes.

4 Combine breadcrumbs, parsley, rind and remaining oil in a small bowl; season. Press mixture onto fish.

5 Remove dish from oven. Place fish on top of kumara; roast, uncovered, about 20 minutes or until kumara is golden and fish is just cooked through. Stand 5 minutes before sprinkling with extra coriander. Serve with lemon cheeks, if you like.

serving suggestion Serve with a cucumber and coriander (cilantro) salad.

tip You can use any firm white fish fillet you like. Blue-eye trevalla or thick snapper fillets would work well.

Healthy
CHOICE

LAMB & EGGPLANT PIES
with fetta crust

PREP & COOK TIME 1 HOUR **SERVES** 6

2 tablespoons olive oil
1 large eggplant (450g), chopped coarsely
1 large brown onion (200g), chopped finely
3 cloves garlic, crushed
1kg (2 pounds) minced (ground) lamb
1 teaspoon ground cinnamon
½ teaspoon ground allspice
1½ cups (375ml) beef stock
2 tablespoons tomato paste
2 tablespoons finely chopped fresh oregano
2 tablespoons finely chopped fresh mint
¼ cup (20g) finely grated parmesan

fetta crust

475g (15-ounce) tub mashed potato
200g (6½ ounces) fetta, crumbled

1 Heat half the oil in a large saucepan over medium-high heat; cook eggplant, stirring, for 5 minutes or until tender. Remove from pan.

2 Heat remaining oil in same pan; cook onion and garlic, stirring, for 3 minutes or until onion softens. Add lamb; cook, stirring, for 5 minutes or until browned. Add spices; cook, stirring, for 1 minute or until fragrant. Add stock and paste; bring to the boil. Reduce heat; simmer, for 20 minutes or until thickened slightly. Remove from heat; stir in herbs and eggplant. Season to taste.

3 Meanwhile, make fetta crust.

4 Preheat oven to 220°C/425°F. Oil six 1-cup (250ml) ovenproof dishes; place on oven trays.

5 Divide lamb mixture among dishes; top with fetta crust. Sprinkle with parmesan. Bake for 15 minutes or until browned lightly. Serve topped with extra oregano leaves, if you like.

fetta crust Heat mashed potato according to packet directions. Stir in fetta; season to taste.

SPINACH & RICOTTA GNOCCHI
with pumpkin & sage

PREP & COOK TIME 45 MINUTES **SERVES** 4

1 large kumara (orange sweet potato) (500g), chopped coarsely

1 medium red onion (170g), cut into thin wedges

cooking-oil spray

200g (6½ ounces) baby spinach leaves

500g (1 pound) firm fresh ricotta

1 cup (80g) finely grated parmesan

½ cup (75g) plain (all-purpose) flour

2 eggs, beaten lightly

1 tablespoon extra virgin olive oil

80g (2½ ounces) butter, chopped

16 sage leaves

1 Preheat oven to 220°C/425°F.

2 Place kumara and onion on a baking-paper-lined oven tray. Spray with cooking oil; season. Roast for 30 minutes or until golden and tender.

3 Meanwhile, briefly cook spinach in a large saucepan of boiling salted water; drain. Refresh in iced water; drain. Squeeze excess water from spinach; chop finely. Place spinach in a large bowl with ricotta, parmesan, flour, egg and oil; season, then mix well.

4 Bring a large saucepan of salted water to the boil. Shape level tablespoons of spinach mixture into ovals. Drop gnocchi, in batches, into boiling water; cook 1-2 minutes or until gnocchi float to the surface. Using a slotted spoon, remove immediately; drain well.

5 Cook butter and gnocchi in a large frying pan over medium heat until butter and gnocchi have browned. Add sage; remove from heat.

6 Stir kumara and onion into gnocchi mixture to serve.

tips Blanching the spinach in step 3 prevents the spinach from overcooking. Make sure you use firm fresh ricotta otherwise the gnocchi may not hold together. It is available from the deli section of supermarkets. Gnocchi can be prepared several hours ahead. Store, covered, in the fridge. Cook just before serving.

Meat
FREE

Cheap
EAT

CRISP-SKINNED CHICKEN
with tomato-braised beans

PREP & COOK TIME 50 MINUTES **SERVES** 4

600g (1¼ pounds) baby new (chat) potatoes

2 tablespoons olive oil

90g (3 ounces) butter, melted

¼ cup (60ml) lemon juice

3 cloves garlic, crushed

3 teaspoons finely chopped fresh thyme

12 chicken drumsticks (1.8kg)

1 medium brown onion (150g), chopped coarsely

500g (1 pound) green beans, trimmed

3 medium tomatoes (450g), chopped coarsely

¼ cup (60ml) chicken stock

2 teaspoons balsamic glaze

2 medium lemons (280g), halved

fresh thyme sprigs, extra, to serve

1 Preheat oven to 200°C/400°F.

2 Prick potatoes with a fork; microwave on HIGH (100%) for 4 minutes or until tender. Using a clean tea towel, press each potato lightly under the palm of your hand on a board to flatten slightly. Place on an oiled oven tray; drizzle with half the oil, season.

3 Combine butter, juice, garlic and thyme in a small bowl. Brush butter mixture all over chicken; place in an oiled large baking dish. Roast chicken and potatoes for 35 minutes, basting chicken occasionally with pan juices, or until chicken is cooked and potatoes are golden and crisp.

4 Meanwhile, heat remaining oil in a large saucepan over medium-high heat; cook onion, stirring, until onion softens. Add beans, tomato and stock; cook, covered, stirring occasionally, for 20 minutes or until vegetables are soft and saucy. Stir in balsamic glaze; season to taste.

5 Serve chicken with beans, potatoes and lemon; sprinkle with extra thyme.

Spinach & CHEESE SNAILS

Meat
FREE

1

2

3

4

Spinach & CHEESE SNAILS

PREP & COOK TIME 50 MINUTES **SERVES** 4

- **750g (1½ pounds) silver beet (swiss chard), trimmed, chopped coarsely (see tips)**
- **1 tablespoon olive oil**
- **6 green onions (scallions), sliced thinly**
- **2 cloves garlic, crushed**
- **1 cup (200g) low-fat low-salt cottage cheese**
- **⅓ cup finely-chopped fresh mint**
- **⅓ cup finely chopped fresh flat-leaf parsley**
- **2 egg yolks**
- **cooking-oil spray**
- **8 sheets fillo pastry**

tomato salad

- **4 medium roma (egg) tomatoes (150g), cut into wedges**
- **1 small red onion (100g), sliced thinly**
- **2 teaspoons extra virgin olive oil**
- **2 tablespoons fresh oregano leaves**

1 Preheat oven to 180°C/350°F. Grease and line two oven trays with baking paper.

2 Cook silver beet in a large saucepan of boiling water for 5 minutes; drain, rinse under cold water. Squeeze out excess water, place silver beet in a large bowl.

3 Heat oil in a medium frying pan over low heat; cook onion and garlic, stirring occasionally, for 3 minutes or until soft. Add onion mixture to silver beet with cheese, herbs and egg yolks; stir until well combined. Season.

4 Spray one sheet of pastry with oil, top with another sheet. Spoon one-quarter of the silver beet mixture along one long edge of the pastry and roll up tightly to form a sausage shape. Roll pastry to make a snail shape. Place on tray. Repeat with remaining pastry and silver beet mixture to make 4 snails.

5 Spray each snail lightly with oil; bake for 35 minutes or until pastry is crisp and golden.

6 Meanwhile, make tomato salad. Serve snails with salad.

tomato salad Combine ingredients in a medium bowl.

tips You will need 1 bunch silver beet for this recipe. Make the filling a day ahead. The recipe is best baked just before serving.

KUMARA JACKET POTATOES
with sloppy joes

PREP & COOK TIME 50 MINUTES **SERVES** 4

1 tablespoon olive oil

1 small brown onion (80g), chopped finely

1 clove garlic, crushed

1 small carrot (70g), chopped finely

1 small red capsicum (bell pepper) (150g), chopped finely

1 celery stalk (150g), trimmed, chopped finely

500g (1 pound) minced (ground) beef

1 tablespoon mild american-style mustard

½ cup (140g) tomato sauce (ketchup)

⅓ cup (80ml) beef stock

6 small kumara (orange sweet potato) (1.5kg)

⅓ cup (35g) pizza cheese

⅓ cup micro parsley

1 Heat oil in a large saucepan over medium-high heat; cook onion, garlic, carrot, capsicum and celery, stirring, for 5 minutes or until vegetables soften. Increase heat to high, add beef; cook, stirring, for 5 minutes or until browned.

2 Add mustard, sauce and stock to pan; cook, stirring, about 10 minutes or until sauce thickens. Season to taste.

3 Preheat grill (broiler).

4 Scrub kumara; pierce all over with a fork. Wrap separately in plastic wrap; microwave on HIGH (100%) for 10 minutes or until tender. Cool for 5 minutes; remove and discard plastic wrap.

5 For each kumara, cut a 2cm (¾-inch) deep slit lengthways, from one end to the other. Using a tea towel, gently squeeze the base of the kumara to open the top. Place on a foil-lined oven tray. Sprinkle kumara with cheese; grill about 3 minutes or until cheese is melted.

6 Serve kumara topped with beef mixture and parsley.

serving suggestion Serve with a mixed leaf salad.

Lebanese roasted PUMPKIN SALAD

PREP & COOK TIME 45 MINUTES **SERVES** 4

2 tablespoons honey

1 cup (100g) walnuts

2kg (4 pounds) jap pumpkin, cut into 2.5cm (1-inch) thick wedges

1 large red capsicum (bell pepper) (350g), sliced thickly

1 large red onion (300g), cut into thin wedges

2 tablespoons olive oil

400g (12½ ounces) canned lentils, drained, rinsed

60g (2 ounces) watercress, sprigs picked

lebanese spice mix

1 teaspoon sweet paprika

1 teaspoon ground cumin

1 teaspoon ground coriander

½ teaspoon ground cinnamon

yoghurt dressing

½ cup (140g) greek-style yoghurt

¼ cup (60ml) olive oil

1 tablespoon finely grated lemon rind

¼ cup (60ml) lemon juice

1 tablespoon honey

1 Preheat oven to 200°C/400°F. Line three oven trays with baking paper.

2 Make lebanese spice mix.

3 Bring honey to the boil in a small frying pan over medium heat. Add walnuts and 1 teaspoon spice mix; toss gently to coat. Transfer to a tray; set aside to cool.

4 Place pumpkin on another tray, and capsicum and onion on remaining tray. Drizzle with oil and remaining spice mix; toss to coat. Bake for 30 minutes or until capsicum and onions are tender; remove from oven.

5 Meanwhile, make yoghurt dressing.

6 Serve roasted vegetables with lentils, watercress, nuts and yoghurt dressing.

lebanese spice mix Combine ingredients in a small bowl.

yoghurt dressing Combine ingredients in a small bowl; season to taste.

tip Make extra spice mix and store in an airtight container for up to 1 month.

Meat
FREE

Meat
FREE

CARROT FALAFEL
with lemon yoghurt

PREP & COOK TIME 40 MINUTES **SERVES** 4

2 medium carrots (240g), grated coarsely

400g (12½ ounces) canned chickpeas (garbanzo beans), drained, rinsed

1 small red onion (100g), chopped finely

1 teaspoon ground cumin

⅓ cup (50g) plain (all-purpose) flour

½ teaspoon baking powder

1 egg

1½ cups (225g) panko (japanese) breadcrumbs

vegetable oil, for deep-frying

2 baby cos (romaine) lettuce (360g), leaves separated

1 lebanese cucumber (130g), sliced thinly

4 x 20cm (8-inch) wholegrain wraps (70g)

¼ cup fresh flat-leaf parsley leaves

lemon yoghurt

1 small clove garlic, crushed

2 tablespoons lemon juice

¾ cup (200g) greek-style yoghurt

1 tablespoon finely chopped fresh flat-leaf parsley

1 Process carrot, chickpeas, onion, cumin, flour, baking powder and egg until mixture just comes together; season. Transfer carrot mixture to a large bowl; stir in ¾ cup of the breadcrumbs. Roll level tablespoons of carrot mixture into balls (mixture should make about 28). Roll falafel in remaining breadcrumbs to coat.

2 Fill a large saucepan or wok one-third with oil and heat to 180°C/350°F (or until a cube of bread browns in 15 seconds). Deep-fry falafel, in batches, for 2 minutes or until golden and cooked through. Drain on paper towel.

3 Meanwhile, make lemon yoghurt.

4 Combine lettuce and cucumber in a large bowl. Top wraps with salad, falafel and lemon yoghurt; sprinkle with parsley. Serve with lemon wedges, if you like.

lemon yoghurt Combine ingredients in a small bowl; season to taste.

Mini caramelised onion & PROSCIUTTO MEATLOAVES

PREP & COOK TIME 1 HOUR SERVES 6

12 slices prosciutto (120g)

750g (1½ pounds) minced (ground) beef

1 egg

1 cup (70g) stale breadcrumbs

2 tablespoons tomato paste

1 clove garlic, crushed

½ cup (170g) bottled caramelised onion

⅓ cup (95g) tomato sauce (ketchup)

⅓ cup (95g) barbecue sauce

2 tablespoons wholegrain mustard

2 tablespoons light brown sugar

¼ cup (60ml) water

60g (2 ounces) baby rocket (arugula) leaves

parsnip mash

3 medium potatoes (600g), chopped coarsely

2 medium parsnips (500g), chopped coarsely

40g (1½ ounces) butter, chopped coarsely

½ cup (125ml) hot milk

1 Preheat oven to 200°C/400°F. Oil six holes of a eight-hole (⅔-cup/160ml) loaf pan. Line each oiled pan hole with two slices prosciutto, overlapping in a criss-cross pattern.
2 Combine beef, egg, breadcrumbs, paste and garlic in a large bowl; season. Press two-thirds of the beef mixture into pan holes; top with caramelised onion, cover with remaining beef mixture. Fold prosciutto slices over to cover beef mixture.
3 Bake about 15 minutes. Remove from oven. Drain excess juices from pan.
4 Remove loaves from pan; place on a foil-lined oven tray. Combine half the sauces, half the mustard and half the sugar in a small bowl. Brush meatloaves with sauce mixture; bake about 10 minutes or until cooked through, basting with sauce mixture occasionally.
5 Meanwhile, make parsnip mash.
6 To make mustard glaze, combine the water with remaining sauces, mustard and sugar in a small saucepan; stir over low heat until sugar dissolves. Bring to the boil. Reduce heat; simmer, uncovered, 2 minutes.
7 Serve meatloaf with parsnip mash, mustard glaze and rocket leaves.
parsnip mash Boil, steam or microwave potato and parsnip until tender; drain. Mash vegetables in a large bowl with butter and milk until smooth. Season to taste.

CHICKEN & BROCCOLI PIE
with pangrattato topping

PREP & COOK TIME 1 HOUR **SERVES** 4

- **500g (1 pound) broccoli, cut into small florets**
- **40g (1½ ounces) butter**
- **2 tablespoons plain (all-purpose) flour**
- **2 cups (500ml) milk**
- **½ cup (60g) coarsely grated cheddar**
- **2½ cups (400g) shredded barbecued chicken**
- **4 slices sourdough bread (280g)**
- **1 tablespoon olive oil**
- **1 clove garlic, crushed**
- **1 tablespoon finely grated lemon rind**
- **2 tablespoons finely chopped fresh flat-leaf parsley leaves**
- **½ cup (40g) finely grated parmesan**
- **fresh flat-leaf parsley leaves, extra, to serve**

1 Preheat oven to 220°C/425°F. Oil a deep 2-litre (6-cup) ovenproof dish.

2 Cook broccoli in a large saucepan of boing water for 5 minutes or until just tender; drain. Rinse under cold water; drain, cool.

3 Melt butter in same cleaned pan, add flour; cook, stirring, about 2 minutes or until mixture bubbles and thickens. Gradually stir in milk; cook, stirring, until mixture boils and thickens. Stir in cheddar, chicken and broccoli; season. Spoon mixture into dish.

4 Tear bread into pieces; combine bread with remaining ingredients in a medium bowl. Sprinkle bread mixture on top of chicken mixture. Bake about 30 minutes or until browned lightly. Stand 5 minutes. Serve sprinkled with extra parsley.

Mexican beef 'LASAGNE'

PREP & COOK TIME 50 MINUTES SERVES 6

1 tablespoon olive oil

1 large red onion (300g), sliced thinly

1 medium red capsicum (bell pepper) (200g), sliced thinly

400g (12 ½ ounces) minced (ground) beef

800g (1½ pounds) canned diced tomatoes

420g (13½ ounces) canned kidney beans, drained, rinsed

310g (10 ounces) canned corn kernels, drained, rinsed

30g (1 ounce) taco seasoning

⅓ cup coarsely chopped fresh coriander (cilantro)

4 x 19cm (7½-inch) flour tortillas

¾ cup (75g) coarsely grated mozzarella

1 lime, cut into cheeks

avocado salad

1 large avocado (320g), chopped coarsely

125g (4 ounces) grape tomatoes, halved

2 tablespoons lime juice

1 tablespoon coarsely chopped fresh coriander (cilantro)

1 Preheat oven to 220°C/425°F.

2 Heat oil in a large saucepan over medium-high heat; cook onion and capsicum, stirring, about 5 minutes or until tender. Increase heat to high, add beef; cook, stirring, for 5 minutes or until browned. Add tomatoes, beans, corn and seasoning; simmer, for 10 minutes or until thickened slightly. Remove from heat; stir in coriander. Season to taste.

3 Line base and sides of a 20cm (8-inch) round springform pan with foil or baking paper; place on oven tray. Line base of pan with a tortilla; top with one-third of the beef mixture. Repeat layering with remaining tortillas and beef mixture, finishing with a tortilla; sprinkle with cheese. Bake for 20 minutes until browned lightly. Stand 5 minutes before cutting.

4 Meanwhile, make avocado salad. Serve 'lasagne' with avocado salad and lime cheeks.

avocado salad Combine ingredients in a medium bowl; season to taste.

serving suggestion Serve with sour cream.

Dairy
FREE

Paprika lamb & CHICKPEA TRAY BAKE

PREP & COOK TIME 45 MINUTES **SERVES** 4

8 lamb forequarter chops (1.5kg)

1 tablespoon ground turmeric

2 teaspoons smoked paprika

2 teaspoons finely grated lemon rind

1 clove garlic, crushed

⅓ cup (80ml) olive oil

500g (1 pound) cherry truss tomatoes, on the vine

400g (12½ ounces) canned chickpeas (garbanzo beans), drained, rinsed

⅓ cup loosely packed fresh flat-leaf parsley leaves

1 tablespoon lemon juice

1 lemon (140g), cut into wedges

1 Preheat oven to 220°C/425°F. Line a baking dish with baking paper.

2 Combine lamb, turmeric, paprika, rind, garlic and half the oil in dish; season. Spread into a single layer. Roast for 15 minutes.

3 Remove dish from oven, add tomatoes; drizzle with half the remaining oil, season. Return to oven; roast for 15 minutes or until lamb is cooked as desired.

4 Just before serving, add chickpeas, parsley, juice and remaining oil to dish. Serve with lemon wedges.

LENTIL SAUSAGE ROLLS
with tomato sumac salad

PREP & COOK TIME 45 MINUTES **SERVES** 4

2 x 400g (12½ ounces) canned lentils, drained, rinsed
1 small brown onion (80g), grated finely
2 cloves garlic, crushed
⅓ cup (45g) coarsely chopped, roasted pistachios
1 teaspoon sweet paprika
1 teaspoon ground cumin
¼ teaspoon ground cinnamon
1 egg, beaten lightly
10 sheets fillo pastry
cooking-oil spray
½ teaspoon sumac
⅔ cup (190g) greek-style yoghurt

tomato sumac salad

200g (6½ ounces) mixed baby heirloom tomatoes, halved
½ small red onion (50g), sliced thinly
1 tablespoon thin strips lemon rind
100g (3 ounces) mixed baby salad leaves
½ cup fresh flat-leaf parsley leaves
1½ tablespoons olive oil
1½ tablespoons lemon juice
½ teaspoon sumac

1 Preheat oven to 200°C/400°F. Line an oven tray with baking paper.
2 Place lentils in a large bowl; mash lightly. Add onion, garlic, pistachios, paprika, cumin, cinnamon and egg; stir to combine. Season.
3 Layer five sheets of fillo, spraying each sheet with oil (cover remaining fillo sheets with a clean, damp tea towel). Place half the lentil mixture along one long side of fillo; roll to enclose filling. Cut into four even lengths. Place on tray; spray with oil. Repeat with remaining fillo, oil spray and lentil mixture to make 8 rolls in total.
4 Sprinkle rolls with sumac; bake for 30 minutes or until golden and crisp.
5 Meanwhile, make tomato sumac salad.
6 Serve lentil rolls with salad and yoghurt.
tomato sumac salad Place ingredients in a large bowl; toss to combine.

Meat
FREE

Lamb, pomegranate & HUMMUS TARTS

PREP & COOK TIME 1 HOUR SERVES 4

1 sheet puff pastry
1 egg, beaten lightly
¼ cup (60ml) olive oil
2 tablespoons lemon juice
1 clove garlic, crushed
1 tablespoon finely chopped fresh flat-leaf parsley
1 tablespoon finely chopped fresh thyme
375g (12 ounces) lamb eye of loin (backstrap)
4 slices drained chargrilled eggplant (160g)
50g (1½ ounces) baby spinach leaves
¼ cup (30g) pitted kalamata olives, halved lengthways
⅓ cup (80g) pomegranate seeds

hummus

¼ cup (60ml) hot water
1½ tablespoons lemon juice
1 tablespoon olive oil
1 tablespoon tahini
1 clove garlic, chopped finely
1 teaspoon sea salt flakes
400g (12½ ounces) canned chickpeas (garbanzo beans), drained, rinsed

1 Make hummus.
2 Preheat oven to 220°C/425°F.
3 Cut pastry in half. Place pastry on baking-paper-lined oven tray. Prick pastry well with fork; brush pastry lightly with egg. Bake about 15 minutes or until puffed and browned.
4 Combine oil with juice, garlic and herbs in a jug; reserve ¼ cup (60ml) marinade. Pour remaining mixture over lamb in a shallow dish; turn to coat. Season lamb, cook on a heated oiled grill plate, over medium-high heat, for 4 minutes each side or until browned and cooked as desired. Remove from grill; cover, stand for 5 minutes before slicing thinly.
5 Spread hummus thickly over base of tarts, top with eggplant, lamb, spinach, olives and pomegranate; drizzle tarts with the reserved marinade.
hummus Blend ingredients until smooth; season to taste.

tip Use store-bought hummus, or beetroot hummus, if you prefer.

Fennel, lemon, pea
& PRAWN RISOTTO

PREP & COOK TIME 45 MINUTES **SERVES** 4

- **1 litre (4 cups) gluten-free chicken stock**
- **1 cup (250ml) water**
- **90g (3 ounces) butter**
- **1 medium brown onion (150g), chopped finely**
- **1 baby fennel bulb (130g), chopped finely, fronds reserved**
- **½ cup (125ml) dry white wine**
- **1½ cups (300g) arborio rice**
- **½ cup (60ml) frozen peas**
- **1 tablespoon finely grated lemon rind**
- **500g (1 pound) shelled and deveined uncooked medium prawns (shrimp), tails intact**
- **1 clove garlic, crushed**

1 Bring stock and the water to the boil in a medium saucepan. Reduce heat to low; simmer, covered.

2 Meanwhile, heat 60g (2 ounces) of the butter in a large saucepan over medium heat; cook onion and fennel, stirring, for 5 minutes or until tender. Add wine; simmer, for 3 minutes or until reduced by half. Add rice; stir to coat in mixture.

3 Add 1 cup of the hot stock; cook, stirring gently, over medium heat until liquid is absorbed. Continue adding stock in 1-cup batches, stirring, until stock is absorbed after each addition. Total cooking time should be about 25 minutes or until rice is tender. Stir in peas and rind; season to taste.

4 Meanwhile, heat remaining butter in a large frying pan over medium-high heat; cook prawns with garlic, for 2 minutes or until prawns change colour.

5 Serve risotto topped with prawns and reserved fennel fronds. Accompany with lemon wedges and garnish with baby sorrel leaves, if you like.

tip You can buy shelled and deveined prawns from your fishmonger or large supermarkets.

Gluten
FREE

Cheap
EAT

ITALIAN MEATBALLS WITH eggplant puree & tomato salsa

PREP & COOK TIME 45 MINUTES **SERVES** 4

2 medium eggplants (460g)

500g (1 pound) beef and lamb italian-style meatballs

2 cloves garlic, quartered

2 tablespoons tahini

¾ cup (200g) greek-style yoghurt

2 tablespoons lemon juice

100g (3 ounces) rocket (arugula) leaves

2 tablespoons olive oil

4 pitta pocket breads (340g), warmed

1 lemon (140g), cut into wedges

tomato salsa

3 medium tomatoes (450g), chopped coarsely

¼ cup finely chopped fresh mint

2 tablespoons finely chopped fresh flat-leaf parsley

1 Cut eggplant in half lengthways. Using a small knife, cut a criss-cross pattern on the cut side. Cook eggplant, cut-side down, on a heated oiled grill plate (or grill pan or barbecue), for 10 minutes or until tender and soft. Cool slightly.

2 Cook meatballs on same grill plate, turning, for 10 minutes or until browned all over and cooked through. Remove from grill; cover to keep warm.

3 Using a spoon, scoop eggplant flesh from skin. Discard skin. Blend or process eggplant flesh with garlic, tahini, yoghurt and juice until almost smooth; season to taste.

4 Make tomato salsa.

5 Serve meatballs with eggplant puree, rocket and salsa; drizzle with oil. Accompany with pitta and lemon wedges.

tomato salsa Combine ingredients in a medium bowl; season to taste.

Red bean & MUSHROOM NACHOS

PREP & COOK TIME 45 MINUTES **SERVES** 4

- **1 tablespoon olive oil**
- **1 medium brown onion (150g), chopped finely**
- **1 medium red capsicum (bell pepper) (200g), chopped finely**
- **200g (6½ ounces) button mushrooms, sliced thickly**
- **200g (6½ ounces) swiss brown mushrooms, sliced thickly**
- **30g (1 ounce) taco seasoning**
- **400g (12½ ounces) canned kidney beans, drained, rinsed**
- **300g (9½ ounces) canned corn kernels, drained, rinsed**
- **375g (12 ounces) bottled mild thick and chunky salsa**
- **330g (10½ ounces) corn chips**
- **½ cup (50g) pizza cheese**
- **½ cup (125g) guacamole or avocado dip**
- **½ cup (140g) sour cream**
- **½ cup loosely packed fresh coriander (cilantro) sprigs**

1 Heat oil in a large saucepan over medium heat; cook onion, capsicum and mushrooms, stirring, for 5 minutes or until softened. Add taco seasoning; cook, stirring, 1 minute or until fragrant.

2 Add beans, corn, and salsa to pan; bring to the boil. Reduce heat to low; simmer, 5 minutes or until sauce thickens. Season to taste.

3 Meanwhile, preheat grill (broiler).

4 Place corn chips in a large ovenproof dish (or into four ovenproof serving dishes); sprinkle with cheese. Grill about 3 minutes or until cheese melts.

5 Serve corn chips immediately, topped with bean mixture, guacamole, sour cream and coriander.

Meat
FREE

Meat
FREE

Garlicky pumpkin & FETTA QUICHES

PREP & COOK TIME 1 HOUR (PLUS FREEZING) **MAKES** 6

3 sheets shortcrust pastry

900g (1¾ pounds) butternut pumpkin, chopped

3 cloves garlic, crushed

½ cup (125ml) pouring cream

¼ cup coarsely chopped fresh sage

½ cup (60g) frozen peas

3 eggs, beaten lightly

75g (2½ ounces) fetta

1½ tablespoons pine nuts

60g (2 ounces) mixed baby salad leaves

½ cup (140g) beetroot relish

1 Preheat oven to 200°C/400°F. Oil six 9cm x 12cm (3½-inch x 5-inch) oval pie tins.

2 Cut each pastry sheet in half diagonally. Lift pastry triangles into tins; press into side, trim edge. Freeze for 5 minutes.

3 Meanwhile, microwave pumpkin on HIGH (100%) for 8 minutes or until tender. Transfer to a large bowl. Coarsely mash pumpkin and garlic with a fork. Stir in cream, sage, peas and egg; season.

4 Place tins on an oven tray; cover pastry with baking paper, fill with dried beans or rice. Bake 10 minutes. Remove paper and beans; bake for a further 5 minutes or until browned lightly.

5 Fill pastry cases with pumpkin mixture. Sprinkle with crumbled fetta and nuts. Bake for 25 minutes or until set and browned.

6 Serve quiches with salad leaves and relish.

tip Quiches are suitable to freeze for up to 3 months. Defrost in refrigerator overnight before reheating in a moderate oven.

BACON & CORN FRITTERS
with avocado dressing

PREP & COOK TIME 50 MINUTES **SERVES** 4

125g (4 ounces) rindless thick bacon slices, chopped coarsely
125g (4 ounces) canned corn kernels, drained, rinsed
2 cloves garlic, crushed
400g (12½ ounces) ripe tomatoes, chopped finely
2 teaspoons smoked paprika
2 tablespoons chopped fresh chives
2 eggs
⅓ cup (80ml) milk
1 cup (150g) spelt flour
½ teaspoon baking powder
1 medium avocado (250g)
½ cup (150g) whole-egg mayonnaise
1 tablespoon lemon juice
1 clove garlic, crushed, extra
2 tablespoons olive oil
1 large fennel bulb (550g), sliced thinly
1 tablespoon chopped fresh chives, extra

1 Heat a large, non-stick frying pan over high heat; cook bacon until golden and crisp. Transfer to a large bowl.
2 Add corn, garlic, tomato, paprika, chives, egg and milk; stir to combine. Add combined sifted flour and baking powder; season and stir to combine. Stand mixture for 10 minutes.
3 Meanwhile, blend or process avocado flesh, mayonnaise, juice and extra garlic until smooth. Season to taste.
4 Heat oil in same frying pan over medium heat. Spoon 2 tablespoonfuls of batter into pan; cook for 2 minutes or until bubbles appear. Turn fritters; cook until other side is lightly browned. Repeat with remaining mixture to make 8 fritters in total.
5 Combine fennel and extra chives in a small bowl. Season.
6 Serve fritters with fennel salad, avocado mixture and lemon halves, if you like.

Cheap EAT

Express PIZZA DOUGH

PREP TIME 10 MINUTES (PLUS STANDING)
MAKES 2 LARGE ROUND PIZZAS OR 4 INDIVIDUAL PIZZAS

This quantity of pizza dough makes 2 x 30cm (12-inch) round pizzas or 4 x 15cm (6-inch) round individual pizzas.

1½ cups (225g) "00" flour, bread flour or plain (all-purpose) flour

1 teaspoon (4g) dry yeast

1 teaspoon caster (superfine) sugar

1 teaspoon fine table salt

2 tablespoons olive oil

½ cup (125ml) warm water, approximately

1 Preheat oven to 200°C/400°F.

2 Place flour, yeast, sugar and salt in the bowl of a food processor; pulse for a few seconds until combined. With the motor operating, pour in oil and the water, processing until ingredients come together. Process for a further minute or until smooth and elastic. Place dough in a large oiled stainless steel bowl; cover with plastic wrap.

3 Turn the oven off; place the bowl of dough in the turned off oven for 15 minutes or until dough doubles in size. Remove bowl from oven. Use dough to make one of the pizzas on the following pages.

FAST PIZZA

Salami, ricotta & KALE

PREP & COOK TIME 15 MINUTES
SERVES 4

Make pizza dough (page 169). Oil two oven or pizza trays; place in oven then preheat to 240°C/475°F. Divide dough into two portions; roll each portion on a floured surface into a 15cm x 30cm (6-inch x 12-inch) oval. Place dough on trays; spread with ⅓ cup pizza sauce (with herbs and garlic). Top with 150g (4½oz) shaved mild danish salami, 500g (1lb) cherry truss tomatoes, ½ thinly sliced small red onion, ½ cup crumbled ricotta; bake about 15 minutes or until bases are browned and crisp. Serve topped with 60g (2oz) baby kale leaves.

Teriyaki chicken & PINEAPPLE

PREP & COOK TIME 15 MINUTES
SERVES 4

Make pizza dough (page 169). Oil two oven or pizza trays; place in oven then preheat to 240°C/475°F. Divide dough into two portions; roll each portion on a floured surface into a 15cm x 30cm (6-inch x 12-inch) oval. Place dough on trays. Drain a 227g (7oz) can pineapple pieces; drain on paper towel. Combine ⅓ cup barbecue sauce with 2 tablespoons teriyaki sauce in a small jug. Spread two-thirds of the sauce mixture on bases; top with 1½ cups shredded barbecued chicken, 1 thinly sliced small red capsicum, 1 thinly sliced flat mushroom and pineapple. Bake pizzas about 15 minutes or until bases are browned and crisp. Serve drizzled with remaining sauce mixture; sprinkle with 2 thinly sliced green onions (scallions).

Fresh tomato & MOZZARELLA

PREP & COOK TIME 15 MINUTES
SERVES 4

Make pizza dough (page 169). Oil two oven or pizza trays; place in oven then preheat to 240°C/475°F. Divide dough into two portions; roll each portion on a floured surface into a 15cm x 30cm (6-inch x 12-inch) oval. Place dough on trays; spread with ½ cup tomato passata. Bake pizzas for 15 minutes or until bases are browned and crisp. Top pizza bases with 400g (12½oz) thickly sliced mixed baby heirloom tomatoes and 150g (4½oz) torn buffalo mozzarella; drizzle with 1 tablespoon olive oil and 2 teaspoons balsamic vinegar. Sprinkle with 1 tablespoon roasted pine nuts, ¼ cup small fresh basil leaves, ¼ cup shaved parmesan and 1 tablespoon olive oil.

Sweet potato & ROSEMARY

PREP & COOK TIME 15 MINUTES
SERVES 4

Make pizza dough (page 169). Oil two oven or pizza trays; place in oven then preheat to 240°C/475°F. Divide dough into two portions; roll each portion on a floured surface into a 15cm x 30cm (6-inch x 12-inch) oval. Place dough on trays; spread with combined ⅓ cup (80ml) olive oil, 1 crushed garlic clove and 1 tablespoon chopped fresh rosemary. Using a vegetable peeler, mandoline or V-slicer, slice 1 small kumara (orange sweet potato) into paper thin strips. Sprinkle with 100g (3oz) crumbled fetta. Bake pizzas about 15 minutes or until bases are browned and crisp. Serve topped with 50g (1½oz) rocket (arugula) leaves and 1 tablespoon olive oil.

Chargrilled fish with
CRISPY TORTILLA SALAD

PREP & COOK TIME 50 MINUTES **SERVES** 4

- 2 tablespoons olive oil
- 3 x 15cm (6-inch) corn tortillas, cut into thin strips
- 2 trimmed corn cobs (500g)
- 20g (¾ ounce) butter, softened
- 800g (1½ pounds) skinless firm white fish fillets, cut into 3cm (1¼-inch) pieces
- 2 cloves garlic, crushed
- 2 tablespoons lime juice
- ½ teaspoon ground cumin
- 1 teaspoon caster (superfine) sugar
- 1 tablespoon olive oil, extra
- ½ medium iceberg lettuce, cut into wedges
- 6 small radishes (100g), trimmed, sliced very thinly
- 1 medium avocado (250g), sliced thinly
- 1 cup loosely packed fresh coriander (cilantro) leaves
- 1 lime, halved

lime dressing

- 2 tablespoons lime juice
- ¼ cup (60ml) olive oil
- 1 clove garlic, crushed
- 1 teaspoon caster (superfine) sugar

1 Make lime dressing.
2 Heat oil in a medium frying pan over medium heat; fry tortilla strips, in two batches, stirring, for 2 minutes or until golden. Remove with a slotted spoon; drain on paper towel. Season with salt to taste.
3 Brush corn with butter; season. Cook corn on a heated oiled grill plate (or grill or barbecue), turning, for 10 minutes or until browned lightly and just tender. Using a sharp knife, cut kernels from cobs. Place in a small bowl; cover to keep warm.
4 Combine fish, garlic, juice, cumin, sugar and oil in a large bowl; season. Thread fish onto 12 metal skewers. Cook skewers on heated grill plate for 3 minutes, turning halfway, or until just cooked through.
5 Place lettuce, radish, avocado and three-quarters of the coriander in a large bowl; toss gently to combine. Arrange lettuce mixture on a platter; layer with corn, drizzle with dressing.
6 Top salad with tortilla strips and remaining coriander. Serve with skewers and lime halves.
lime dressing Place ingredients in a screw-top jar, season; shake well.

tip The tortilla strips can be prepared a day ahead; cool, then store in an airtight container.

Gluten
FREE

Dairy
FREE

Saltimbocca CUTLETS

PREP & COOK TIME 50 MINUTES SERVES 4

¼ cup (60ml) olive oil

2 teaspoons finely grated lemon rind

1 clove garlic, crushed

2 large potatoes (600g), chopped coarsely

400g (12½ ounces) baby (dutch) carrots, trimmed

500g (1 pound) cherry truss tomatoes, on the vine

2 tablespoons dijon mustard

4 veal cutlets (1kg)

8 fresh sage leaves

4 slices prosciutto (60g)

¼ cup (60ml) balsamic vinegar

¾ cup (180ml) chicken stock

1 Preheat oven to 200°C/400°F.

2 Combine 1 tablespoon of the oil with rind, garlic, potato and carrots in a large baking dish; season. Roast vegetables for 30 minutes or until golden and tender.

3 Meanwhile, place tomatoes on a baking-paper-lined oven tray. Drizzle with 2 teaspoons of the oil; season. Roast for last 10 minutes of vegetable cooking time or until skins start to split.

4 Spread mustard on one side of each veal cutlet; top each with 2 sage leaves. Wrap a slice of prosciutto around each cutlet; secure with a toothpick.

5 Heat remaining oil in a large frying pan over medium heat; cook veal for 5 minutes each side or until browned and cooked through. Remove from pan, cover; rest 5 minutes.

6 Add vinegar to same pan; simmer for 2 minutes or until syrupy. Stir in stock; simmer for 3 minutes or until liquid is reduced by half. Serve veal with vegetables and tomatoes; drizzle with sauce.

tip You could also make the recipe with 4 chicken breasts instead of veal cutlets, cooking them for about the same amount of time.

Zucchini schnitzel & SLAW WRAPS

PREP & COOK TIME 40 MINUTES **SERVES** 4

2 medium zucchini (240g), sliced thinly, lengthways

2 free-range eggs, beaten lightly

1⅓ cups (200g) panko (japanese) breadcrumbs

¼ cup (60ml) olive oil

1 green oak leaf lettuce, leaves separated

4 x 20cm (8-inch) wholegrain wraps (70g)

white barbecue sauce

¼ teaspoon garlic powder

¼ teaspoon cayenne pepper

2 teaspoons horseradish cream

⅓ cup (100g) whole-egg mayonnaise

1 tablespoon lemon juice

1 tablespoon water

slaw

1 cup (80g) finely shredded red cabbage

3 green onions (scallions), sliced thinly

1 medium carrot (120g), cut into ribbons

⅔ cup (50g) crunchy sprout combo

1 Make white barbecue sauce, then the slaw.

2 Dip zucchini in egg, then coat in breadcrumbs, pressing lightly to secure.

3 Heat half the oil in a large frying pan over medium-high heat; cook half the zucchini for 3 minutes or until both sides are golden and tender. Repeat with remaining oil and zucchini.

4 Place lettuce along centre of each wrap; top evenly with slaw, zucchini and remaining white barbecue sauce. Roll to enclose filling.

white barbecue sauce Stir ingredients in a small bowl.

slaw Place cabbage, onion, carrot, sprouts and half the white barbecue sauce in a medium bowl; toss to combine. Season to taste.

Meat
FREE

Cheap
EAT

SALMON CAKES
with apple salad

PREP & COOK TIME 50 MINUTES (& FREEZING) **SERVES** 4

415g (13 ounces) canned pink salmon

½ cup (150g) whole-egg mayonnaise

1 teaspoon finely grated lemon rind

475g (15-ounce) tub mashed potato

2 tablespoons finely chopped fresh chives

⅓ cup (35g) plain (all-purpose) flour

2 eggs, beaten lightly

1 cup (75g) panko (japanese) breadcrumbs

60g (2 ounces) ghee

1 medium lemon (140g), cut into wedges

½ cup (150g) aïoli

apple salad

2 tablespoons white wine vinegar

⅓ cup (80ml) olive oil

1 teaspoon dijon mustard

2 medium green-skinned apples (300g), cut into matchsticks

1 bunch red radishes, sliced thinly

1½ cups packed fresh coriander leaves (cilantro)

1 Make apple salad.

2 Drain salmon; discard skin and bones, flake salmon. Drain on paper towel.

3 Stir mayonnaise and rind in a medium bowl; stir in salmon, potato and chives, season. Shape mixture into 8 patties. Place flour, egg and breadcrumbs, separately in shallow bowls. Dust patties in flour, shake away excess. Dip in egg, then coat in breadcrumbs. Place on tray; freeze for 10 minutes until firm but not frozen.

4 Heat ghee in a large frying pan over medium heat; cook patties, in batches, about 4 minutes each side or until golden. Drain on paper towel.

5 Serve salmon cakes with apple salad, lemon wedges and aïoli.

apple salad Whisk vinegar, oil and mustard in a medium bowl until combined. Add apple, radish and coriander; toss gently to combine, season to taste.

BEEF & ROSEMARY PIES

with scone topping

PREP & COOK TIME 55 MINUTES **MAKES** 4

- 2 teaspoons olive oil
- 5 thick beef sausages (750g)
- 1 medium brown onion (150g), chopped finely
- 1 tablespoon plain (all-purpose) flour
- 1¼ cups (310ml) chicken stock
- 1 tablespoon honey
- 2 tablespoons coarsely chopped fresh rosemary
- ½ cup (60g) frozen peas
- 1 tablespoon milk
- 4 sprigs fresh rosemary

scone topping

- 1 cup (150g) self-raising flour
- 60g (2 ounces) butter, chopped coarsely
- ¼ cup (20g) finely grated parmesan
- ½ cup (125ml) milk, approximately

1 Preheat oven to 200°C/400°F. Oil four 1¼-cup (310ml) ovenproof dishes.

2 Heat oil in a large frying pan over medium-high heat; cook sausages until browned and cooked through. Remove from pan; slice thinly.

3 Cook onion in same pan, stirring, for 3 minutes or until softened. Add flour; cook, stirring, for 2 minutes or until mixture bubbles and thickens. Stir in stock, honey and chopped rosemary; cook, stirring, until mixture boils and thickens. Stir in peas; simmer for 3 minutes. Return sausage to pan. Season.

4 Meanwhile, make scone topping.

5 Spoon hot filling into dishes. Top with scone topping. Brush with milk; press a rosemary sprig into top of each pie. Bake about 25 minutes or until golden. Serve with tomato sauce (ketchup), if you like.

scone topping Place flour in a medium bowl; rub in butter, stir in parmesan. Stir in enough milk to make a soft sticky dough. Divide dough into four, knead into rounds to fit dishes.

Balsamic honey SHREDDED BEEF BUNS

PREP & COOK TIME 50 MINUTES **MAKES** 4

- 3 teaspoons olive oil
- 1 small brown onion (80g), chopped finely
- 2 cloves garlic, crushed
- 1 cup (250ml) balsamic vinegar
- ½ cup (140g) tomato sauce (ketchup)
- 1 tablespoon worcestershire sauce
- ¼ cup (55g) firmly packed light brown sugar
- 1 cup (250ml) beef stock
- 2 tablespoons honey
- 1 tablespoon dijon mustard
- 250g (8 ounces) packaged slow cooked pulled bbq beef
- 4 brioche buns (280g), split

cabbage and radish coleslaw

- 200g (6½ ounces) cabbage, sliced thinly
- 4 trimmed radishes (60g), sliced thinly
- 2 tablespoons finely chopped fresh chives
- ¾ cup (150g) mayonnaise
- 2 tablespoons white wine vinegar

1 Make cabbage and radish coleslaw.

2 Heat oil in a large saucepan over medium heat; cook onion and garlic, stirring, until softened. Add vinegar, sauces, sugar, stock, honey and mustard; bring to the boil. Reduce heat to low; simmer, for 20 minutes, stirring occasionally, or until reduced by half and syrupy. Season to taste.

3 Heat beef according to packet directions; stir beef through barbecue sauce. Sandwich buns with shredded beef and coleslaw.

cabbage and radish coleslaw Combine ingredients in a large bowl; season to taste. Refrigerate until required.

tips Packaged pre-cooked shredded slow cooked beef is available from the refrigerated section of large supermarkets (near the fresh meats). You could use packaged shredded slow cooked pork or shredded barbecued chicken for this recipe. You could use 2 thinly sliced celery sticks instead of the radish, if you prefer.

FISH FINGERS WITH *mushy minted peas*

PREP & COOK TIME 50 MINUTES (PLUS FREEZING) **SERVES** 4

1kg (2 pounds) skinless firm white fish fillets, chopped coarsely

2 tablespoons coarsely chopped fresh flat-leaf parsley

2 teaspoons finely grated lemon rind

1 tablespoon lemon juice

1 clove garlic, quartered

½ cup (75g) plain (all-purpose) flour

2 eggs, beaten lightly

1 cup (75g) panko (japanese) breadcrumbs

vegetable oil, for shallow-frying

2 cups (250g) frozen peas

1 tablespoon extra virgin olive oil

2 tablespoons finely chopped fresh mint, plus extra leaves to serve

1 Oil 20cm x 30cm (8-inch x 12-inch) rectangular slice pan.

2 Process fish, parsley, rind, juice and garlic until smooth; season. Using spatula, press mixture evenly into pan; turn onto baking-paper-lined tray. Cut into eight 20cm (8-inch) long slices; cut each slice in half crossways to make 16 fingers. Cover; freeze for 10 minutes or until firm but not frozen.

3 Place flour, egg and breadcrumbs, separately, in three shallow bowls. Pat fish fingers with flour; shake off excess. Dip in egg, then in breadcrumbs.

4 Heat 1cm (½-inch) vegetable oil in a large frying pan over medium heat. Cook fish fingers, in batches, about 4 minutes each side or until golden and cooked through. Remove with a slotted spoon; drain on paper towel.

5 Meanwhile, boil, steam or microwave peas until tender; drain. Coarsely crush peas in a medium bowl; stir in olive oil and mint.

6 Serve fish fingers with mushy minted peas. Accompany with extra mint, tartare sauce or mayonnaise, and lemon wedges, if you like.

tip This recipe is a great way to get kids to eat fish; it's cleverly disguised and tastes great too.

Healthy
CHOICE

Spanish chicken,
CHORIZO AND RICE SOUP

PREP & COOK TIME 50 MINUTES SERVES 4

- **30g (1 ounce) butter**
- **1 small brown onion (80g), chopped finely**
- **2 cloves garlic, crushed**
- **1 medium red capsicum (bell pepper) (200g), chopped finely**
- **2 teaspoons dried oregano**
- **1 teaspoon sweet paprika**
- **1 teaspoon ground cumin**
- **1 tablespoon plain (all-purpose) flour**
- **2 tablespoons tomato paste**
- **1 litre (4 cups) chicken stock**
- **2 cups (500ml) water**
- **400g (12½ ounces) canned crushed tomatoes**
- **½ cup (100g) white medium-grain rice**
- **1 cured chorizo sausage (170g), sliced thinly**
- **2 cups (320g) shredded barbecued chicken**
- **1 large avocado (320g), chopped finely**
- **½ cup coarsely chopped fresh coriander (cilantro)**
- **2 limes, halved**

1 Melt butter in a large saucepan over medium heat; cook onion and garlic, stirring, for 5 minutes or until onion softens. Add capsicum, oregano and spices; cook, stirring, until fragrant. Add flour and paste; cook, stirring, for 1 minute. Gradually stir in stock, the water and tomatoes; bring to the boil, stirring. Stir in rice; simmer, uncovered, stirring occasionally, for 15 minutes or until rice is tender.

2 Meanwhile, heat a large oiled frying pan over medium-high heat; cook chorizo until browned. Drain on paper towel.

3 Add chorizo and chicken to soup; stir over medium heat until hot. Season to taste.

4 Serve bowls of soup topped with avocado, coriander and accompany with lime halves.

Chicken, brie & CRANBERRY PIES

PREP & COOK TIME 45 MINUTES **SERVES** 4

1 tablespoon olive oil

400g (12½ ounces) chicken tenderloins

4 sheets shortcrust pastry

⅔ cup (200g) cranberry sauce, plus extra to serve

300g (¾ ounce) baby spinach leaves

200g (6½ ounces) brie, sliced thinly

1 egg, beaten lightly

½ small red onion (50g), sliced thinly

2 lebanese cucumber (260g), cut into ribbons

2 tablespoons roasted pine nuts

⅓ cup (80ml) french dressing

1 Preheat oven to 220°C/425°F. Line two oven trays with baking paper.

2 Heat oil in a medium frying pan over medium-high heat; season chicken. Cook chicken about 10 minutes or until browned and cooked through. Remove from pan; slice thinly. Cool.

3 Cut eight 10cm (4-inch) rounds from one sheet of pastry. Place rounds on trays. Spread with sauce, leaving 1cm (½-inch) border. Top with 20g (¾ ounce) spinach, chicken and cheese. Brush edges with a little egg. Cut eight 11cm (4½-inch) rounds from remaining pastry sheet. Cover filling; press pastry edges with a fork to seal.

4 Brush pastries with egg. Cut a small slit in centre of each pie. Bake about 20 minutes or until browned lightly.

5 Meanwhile, combine remaining spinach with red onion, cucumber, nuts and dressing in a large bowl; season.

6 Serve pies with extra cranberry sauce and salad.

tip To save time, you could use 1½ cups shredded barbecued chicken instead of cooking the chicken yourself.

Cheap
EAT

EXPRESS SWEETS

Sumac strawberry PAVLOVAS

PREP TIME 10 MINUTES (PLUS REFRIGERATION) **SERVES** 4

250g (8 ounces) strawberries, thinly sliced into rounds (see tip)

⅓ cup (55g) icing (confectioners') sugar

1 tablespoon sumac

300ml thickened (heavy) cream

1 teaspoon vanilla bean paste

4 pavlova nests (240g)

1 Combine strawberries, sifted icing sugar and sumac in a small bowl, cover; refrigerate for 30 minutes.

2 Just before serving, beat cream and vanilla in a small bowl with an electric mixer until firm peaks form. Spoon cream equally among pavlovas; top with sumac strawberries. Serve immediately.

tip Don't slice the strawberries too thinly or they will fall apart during refrigeration.

Lamington cream
LAYER CAKE

PREP TIME 30 MINUTES **SERVES** 8

300ml thickened (heavy) cream

460g (14½-ounce) packaged double unfilled chocolate sponge cake rounds

½ cup (160g) strawberry jam

453g (14½-ounce) tub milk chocolate frosting

1½ cups (120g) shredded coconut

1 Beat cream in a small bowl with an electric mixer until firm peaks form.

2 Split sponge cakes in half. Place one cake layer on board; spread with 2 tablespoons of the jam. Top with one-third of the cream, leaving a 1cm (½-inch) border; top with another cake layer. Repeat layering with remaining jam, cream and cake layers, finishing with a cake layer.

3 Spread side of cake with three-quarters of the frosting. Place coconut on a tray. Holding top and bottom of cake, roll side of cake in coconut.

4 Spread remaining frosting over top of cake; press remaining coconut all over top of cake.

Waffles A LA SUZETTE

PREP & COOK TIME 20 MINUTES SERVES 4

125g (4 ounces) butter

½ cup (110g) caster (superfine) sugar

2 teaspoons finely grated orange rind

½ cup (125ml) orange juice

8 belgian-style waffles (480g)

2 medium oranges (480g), peeled, sliced thinly into rounds

2 cups (500ml) vanilla ice-cream

2 tablespoons toasted flaked almonds

1 To make suzette sauce, melt butter in a small heavy-based saucepan, add sugar, rind and juice; cook, stirring, over low heat, without boiling, until sugar dissolves. Bring to the boil. Reduce heat; simmer, uncovered, without stirring, for 2 minutes or until sauce thickens slightly.

2 Warm waffles according to packet directions.

3 Divide waffles and orange slices among serving plates; top with ice-cream, suzette sauce and almonds.

Gluten
FREE

Pink lemonade FOOLS

PREP & COOK TIME 15 MINUTES (PLUS COOLING) **SERVES** 4

- **250g (8 ounces) strawberries, hulled**
- **⅓ cup (80ml) lemonade**
- **300ml thickened (heavy) cream**
- **⅓ cup (110g) gluten-free lemon curd**
- **⅓ cup (15g) toasted coconut flakes**
- **1½ cups (6g) pink persian fairy floss**
- **1 tablespoon toasted coconut flakes, extra**

1 Thinly slice 4 strawberries into rounds; quarter remaining strawberries. Place quartered strawberries and lemonade in a small frying pan over high heat; bring to the boil. Reduce heat; simmer for 5 minutes, mashing with a fork a few times during cooking, or until strawberries soften slightly and liquid thickens slightly. Cool.

2 Meanwhile, beat cream in a small bowl with an electric mixer until soft peaks form. Fold curd and coconut into cream. Spoon three-quarters of the strawberry mixture onto cream mixture; do not stir.

3 Spoon cream mixture into four ⅔-cup (160ml) glasses. Top with remaining strawberry mixture, reserved sliced strawberries, fairy floss and extra coconut.

Charred peaches with
BERRY ROSEWATER YOGHURT

PREP & COOK TIME 15 MINUTES SERVES 4

6 medium peaches (900g), halved, stones removed

2 tablespoons coarsely chopped pistachios

berry rosewater yoghurt

150g (4½ ounces) strawberries, sliced

1 tablespoon rosewater

1 cup (280g) low-fat vanilla yoghurt

1 Make berry rosewater yoghurt.

2 Heat an oiled grill plate (or grill or barbecue); cook peaches, cut-side down, for 5 minutes or until charred and tender.

3 Divide peaches between serving plates. Spoon yoghurt over peaches; sprinkle with pistachios.

berry rosewater yoghurt Blend or process strawberries with rosewater until smooth. Swirl through yoghurt.

tips You can use thawed frozen strawberries or raspberries for this recipe, and either white or yellow peaches. If peaches are unavailable you could use mango cheeks, pineapple wedges, small ripe pear halves or thick apple slices. For a nut-free version replace the pistachios with toasted flaked coconut or pepitas (pumpkin seed kernels), or you can omit them altogether; it will be equally delicious.

Healthy
CHOICE

Cheap
EAT

Choc-hazelnut BANANA PIES

PREP & COOK TIME 25 MINUTES (PLUS COOLING) MAKES 18

18 (220g) butternut snap biscuits

½ cup (125ml) thickened (heavy) cream

220g (7-ounce) jar chocolate-hazelnut spread

1 medium banana (200g), sliced thinly

2 tablespoons finely chopped roasted hazelnuts

1 Preheat oven to 160°C/325°F. Grease 18 holes of two 12-hole (1½-tablespoons/30ml) shallow round-based patty pans.

2 Place one biscuit over top of each greased pan hole; bake about 4 minutes or until biscuits soften. Using the back of a teaspoon, gently push softened biscuits into pan holes; cool.

3 Beat cream in a small bowl with an electric mixer until soft peaks form.

4 Spoon chocolate-hazelnut spread into pie cases; top each with a slice of banana. Top with cream; sprinkle with nuts.

MELON SALAD
with lime & mint ice

PREP TIME 20 MINUTES **SERVES** 4

½ large pineapple (1kg), peeled, sliced thinly

½ medium rockmelon (850g), peeled, sliced thinly

1.2kg (2½-pound) piece seedless watermelon, peeled, sliced thinly

¼ cup small fresh mint leaves

lime and mint ice

⅓ cup finely chopped fresh mint

2 tablespoons icing (confectioners') sugar

1 tablespoon lime juice

2 cups ice cubes

1 Layer fruit on serving plates.

2 Just before serving, make lime and mint ice.

3 Serve melon salad sprinkled with lime and mint ice; sprinkle with mint.

lime and mint ice Blend or process all ingredients until ice is crushed.

Healthy
CHOICE

Cheap
EAT

Coconut BANANA FRITTERS

PREP & COOK TIME 30 MINUTES **SERVES** 4

- **¼ cup (40g) icing (confectioners') sugar**
- **2 teaspoons ground cinnamon**
- **1 egg**
- **¾ cup (50g) panko (japanese) breadcrumbs**
- **¼ cup (20g) shredded coocnut**
- **vegetable oil, for deep-frying**
- **4 large bananas (920g), halved lengthways**
- **2 cups (500ml) coconut ice-cream (see tips)**

1 Combine sugar and cinnamon in a shallow bowl. Beat egg in another shallow bowl; combine breadcrumbs and coconut in another shallow bowl.

2 Fill a large saucepan or wok one-third with oil and heat to 180°C/350°F (or until a cube of bread browns in 15 seconds). Dip banana in sugar mixture: shake off excess. Dip banana in egg, then in crumb mixture to coat. Deep-fry bananas, in batches, for 2 minutes or until golden. Drain on paper towel.

3 Serve fritters with ice-cream.

tips To make your own coconut ice-cream, soften 2 cups (500ml) of good-quality vanilla ice-cream, then fold in ½ cup toasted shredded coconut and 1 tablespoon coconut-flavoured liqueur or ½ teaspoon coconut essence. Return to the freezer until firm enough to scoop. You could use coconut yoghurt instead of ice-cream, if you prefer.

Chocolate custard
TARTS WITH BERRIES

1

2

3

4

CHOCOLATE CUSTARD TARTS
with fresh berries

PREP & COOK TIME 40 MINUTES (PLUS COOLING) **MAKES** 6

- **3 egg yolks**
- **½ cup (110g) caster (superfine) sugar**
- **2 tablespoons cornflour (cornstarch)**
- **1 tablespoon cocoa powder**
- **¾ cup (180ml) milk**
- **⅔ cup (160ml) pouring cream**
- **1 sheet puff pastry**
- **150g (4½ ounces) fresh raspberries**
- **150g (4½ ounces) fresh blueberries**
- **1 tablespoon icing (confectioners') sugar**

1 Preheat oven to 220°C/425°F. Grease six holes of a 12-hole (⅓ cup/80ml) muffin pan.

2 Combine egg yolks, caster sugar, cornflour and cocoa in a medium saucepan; whisk in milk and cream until smooth. Stir over medium heat until mixture boils and thickens; transfer to a heatproof bowl, cover surface with plastic wrap. Cool.

3 Meanwhile, cut pastry sheet in half; stack two halves, press firmly. Roll pastry up tightly from short side; cut log into six slices. Roll slices between sheets of baking paper into 12cm (4¾-inch) rounds; press rounds into pan holes.

4 Pour custard into pastry cases; bake about 20 minutes or until set. Cool in pan.

5 Serve tarts topped with berries; dust with sifted icing sugar.

Peanut butter CHEESECAKE CUPS

PREP & COOK TIME 20 MINUTES (PLUS COOLING & REFRIGERATION) **SERVES** 4

125g (4 ounces) chocolate chip biscuits

½ cup (140g) crunchy peanut butter

⅓ cup (80ml) thickened (heavy) cream

125g (4 ounces) cream cheese, softened

2 tablespoons icing (confectioners') sugar

125g (4 ounces) almond brittle, chopped coarsely

choc-fudge sauce

100g (3 ounces) dark eating (semi-sweet) chocolate, chopped coarsely

10g (½ ounce) butter

¼ cup (60ml) thickened (heavy) cream

1 Make choc-fudge sauce.

2 Process biscuits until finely chopped. Divide biscuit crumbs between four ¾-cup (180ml) serving glasses.

3 Make filling by combining peanut butter and cream in a small saucepan; stir, over low heat until smooth. Cool.

4 Beat cheese and sugar in a small bowl with electric mixer until smooth. Stir in peanut butter mixture. Spoon filling into glasses. Refrigerate for 20 minutes.

5 Serve cheesecake cups drizzled with choc-fudge sauce; top with almond brittle.

choc-fudge sauce Combine ingredients in a small saucepan; stir over low heat until smooth. Cool.

4-ingredient

TRIPLE CHOC BROWNIES

PREP & COOK TIME 40 MINUTES **MAKES** 16

4 eggs, at room temperature

220g (7-ounce) jar chocolate-hazelnut spread

¼ cup (45g) milk choc bits

¼ cup (45g) white choc bits

1 Preheat oven to 180°C/350°F. Grease a 20cm (8-inch) square cake pan; line base and sides with baking paper, extending paper 5cm (2 inches) over sides.

2 Beat eggs in a medium bowl with an electric mixer on high speed for 10 minutes or until stiff peaks form.

3 Meanwhile, place chocolate-hazelnut spread in a large microwave-safe bowl; microwave on HIGH (100%) for 20 seconds or until softened slightly.

4 Fold egg mixture into chocolate-hazelnut mixture, in three batches. Pour mixture into pan; bake 15 minutes. Remove from oven; sprinkle with combined choc bits. Bake a further 10 minutes or until a skewer inserted into centre comes out clean. Cool in pan before cutting.

tip Brownies will keep at room temperature, in an airtight container, for up to 3 days.

Gluten
FREE

Gluten
FREE

Passionfruit, lemon & COCONUT TARTS

PREP & COOK TIME 30 MINUTES (PLUS COOLING) **MAKES** 12

1 cup (80g) desiccated coconut

1 egg white, beaten lightly

2 tablespoons caster (superfine) sugar

2 tablespoons thickened (heavy) cream

½ cup (160g) gluten-free lemon curd

2 tablespoons passionfruit pulp

1 Preheat oven to 150°C/300°F. Grease 12-hole (2-tablespoon/40ml) mini muffin pan.

2 Combine coconut, egg white and sugar in a medium bowl. Press mixture firmly and evenly over bases and sides of pan holes. Bake about 20 minutes or until browned lightly. Cool; remove from pan.

3 Meanwhile, beat cream in a small bowl with an electric mixer until soft peaks form; fold lemon curd into cream.

4 Divide lemon mixture among coconut cases; top each with a little passionfruit pulp.

Apple pie DOUGHNUTS A LA MODE

PREP & COOK TIME 15 MINUTES **SERVES** 4

6 cinnamon doughnuts (510g)

1 medium red-skinned apple (150g), cored, sliced thickly into rounds

1 medium green-skinned apple (150g), cored, sliced thickly into rounds

½ cup (125ml) pure maple syrup

2 cups (500ml) vanilla ice-cream

1 Split doughnuts in half horizontally. Brush apple slices with 1 tablespoon of the maple syrup.

2 Cook doughnuts and apple slices, in batches, on a heated oiled grill plate (or grill or barbecue) until browned lightly both sides and apple is tender.

3 Stack doughnuts and apple slices on serving plates; top with ice-cream. Drizzle with remaining maple syrup.

tip This 4-ingredient dessert is so simple and versatile; you can use pear, figs, pineapple rings or stone fruit instead of the apple.

Cheap
EAT

Healthy
CHOICE

Dark chocolate & RICOTTA MOUSSE

PREP & COOK TIME 20 MINUTES (PLUS COOLING) **SERVES** 6

- **⅓ cup (110g) rice malt syrup**
- **1 tablespoon dutch-processed cocoa**
- **2 tablespoons water**
- **½ teaspoon vanilla extract**
- **200g (6½ ounces) dark chocolate (70% cocoa), chopped coarsely**
- **8 fresh dates (160g), pitted**
- **½ cup (125ml) milk**
- **2 cups (480g) soft ricotta**
- **150g (4½ ounces) fresh raspberries or pitted fresh cherries**
- **12 fresh dates (240g), extra, halved, seeds removed**

1 Stir syrup, cocoa, the water and extract in a small saucepan over medium heat; bring to the boil. Remove from heat; cool.

2 Place chocolate in a small heatproof bowl over a small saucepan of simmering water (don't let the water touch the base of the bowl); stir until melted and smooth.

3 Process dates and milk until dates are finely chopped. Add ricotta; process until smooth. Add melted chocolate; process until well combined.

4 Spoon mousse into six ¾-cup (180ml) serving glasses. Serve topped with raspberries and extra dates; drizzled with cocoa syrup.

tip Unlike most mousse recipes this can be served immediately. If you wish to make it a day ahead, refrigerate, covered, then bring to room temperature before serving.

FAST

ICE-CREAM SANDWICHES

Pretzel CARAMEL

PREP TIME 20 MINUTES (PLUS FREEZING)
MAKES 4

Place 4 choc wheaten biscuits, chocolate-side down on board. Working one at a time, top each biscuit with a scoop of salted caramel or toffee ice-cream, then sandwich with another choc wheaten biscuit, chocolate-side up. Place on a tray lined with plastic wrap; freeze for 10 minutes. Place 1 cup of salted pretzels in a plastic ziptop bag; pound with a rolling pin until coarsely crushed. Place in a shallow bowl. Working one at a time, roll sides of ice-cream sandwiches in pretzels. Serve immediately or freeze until required.

Loaded TRIPLE CHOC

PREP TIME 20 MINUTES (PLUS FREEZING)
MAKES 4

Place 4 chocolate chip biscuits, rounded-side down on board. Working one at a time, top each biscuit with a scoop of chocolate ice-cream, then sandwich with another chocolate chip biscuit, rounded-side up. Place on a tray lined with plastic wrap; freeze for 10 minutes. Place ½ cup of mini M&Ms in a shallow bowl. Working one at a time, roll sides of ice-cream sandwiches in M&Ms. Serve immediately or freeze until required.

IF YOU HAVE THE TIME, SPREAD THE ICE-CREAM INTO A SLICE PAN LINED WITH PLASTIC WRAP AND FREEZE UNTIL FIRM; CUT ROUNDS FROM ICE-CREAM USING A COOKIE CUTTER.

Minty CRISP

PREP TIME 20 MINUTES (PLUS FREEZING)
MAKES 4

Place 4 mint patties rounded-side down on board. Working one at a time, top each biscuit with a scoop of mint choc chip ice-cream, then sandwich with another mint pattie, rounded-side up. Place on a tray lined with plastic wrap; freeze 10 minutes. Finely chop 2 x 35g (1oz) peppermint crisp bars; place in a shallow bowl. Working one at a time, roll sides of ice-cream sandwiches in peppermint crisp. Serve immediately or freeze until required.

Fruity FIZZ

PREP TIME 20 MINUTES (PLUS FREEZING)
MAKES 4

Place 4 pink tic toc biscuits, icing-side down on board. Working one at a time, top each biscuit with a scoop of berry swirl ice-cream, then sandwich with another pink tic toc biscuit, icing-side up. Place on a tray lined with plastic wrap; freeze 10 minutes. Place 1 x 35g (1oz) packet fruit tingles in a plastic ziptop bag; pound with a rolling pin until coarsely crushed. Place in a shallow bowl. Working one at a time, roll sides of ice-cream sandwiches in fruit tingles. Serve immediately or freeze until required.

Choc-cranberry RICOTTA TARTS

PREP & COOK TIME 35 MINUTES (& COOLING) **MAKES** 12

1½ cups (360g) ricotta

½ cup (110g) caster (superfine) sugar

1 egg, beaten lightly

90g (3 ounces) finely chopped dark (semi-sweet) eating chocolate

⅓ cup (45g) dried cranberries, chopped

¼ cup (40g) sultanas

3 sheets butter puff pastry

1 tablespoon milk

1 tablespoon icing (confectioners') sugar

40g (1½ ounces) dark (semi-sweet) eating chocolate, grated finely

1 Preheat oven to 200°C/400°F. Line oven trays with baking paper.

2 Combine cheese, caster sugar and egg in a medium bowl. Stir in chopped chocolate and dried fruit.

3 Cut 12 x 11cm (4½-inch) rounds from pastry; place rounds on trays. Divide ricotta mixture among rounds, leaving a 2.5cm (1-inch) border. Fold pastry edge up, pinching to seal. Brush pastry with milk; bake tarts for 12 minutes or until browned. Cool for 5 minutes before dusting with sifted icing sugar and sprinkling with grated chocolate.

BANANA PANCAKES
with choc-peanut sauce

PREP & COOK TIME 35 MINUTES **SERVES** 4

1 cup (150g) self-raising flour
2 tablespoons caster (superfine) sugar
1¼ cups (310ml) buttermilk
1 egg, beaten lightly
2 teaspoons pure maple syrup
20g (¾ ounce) butter, melted
1 medium banana (200g), sliced thinly
½ cup (125ml) pouring cream
2 x 60g (2-ounce) Snickers bars, chopped coarsely
2 cups (500ml) chocolate ice-cream

1 Sift flour into a large bowl, stir in sugar. Whisk in combined buttermilk, egg, syrup and butter until batter is smooth. Stir in banana.

2 Heat a large oiled frying pan over medium heat. Pour ¼ cup of the batter into pan, allowing room for spreading. Cook for 2 minutes or until bubbles appear on surface of the pancakes. Turn pancakes; cook for 2 minutes or until browned. Remove from pan, cover to keep warm. Repeat with remaining batter to make a total of 8 pancakes.

3 Meanwhile, heat cream in a small saucepan, add Snickers; stir over low heat until melted.

4 Serve banana pancakes topped with ice-cream and choc-peanut sauce.

COCONUT RICE WITH
mango & raspberries

PREP TIME 15 MINUTES **SERVES** 4

300ml thickened (heavy) cream

½ cup (125ml) coconut cream

½ cup (80g) icing (confectioners') sugar

2¼ cups (340g) cooked medium-grain white rice

1 large mango (600g), sliced thinly

125g (4 ounces) raspberries

½ cup (25g) toasted flaked coconut

1 Beat cream, coconut cream and sugar in a small bowl with an electric mixer until soft peaks form.

2 Place rice in a large bowl; fold in cream mixture. Cover; refrigerate while preparing mango.

3 Blend or process mango until smooth. Divide rice mixture and mango puree, in alternate layers, among four 1-cup (250ml) serving glasses; top with raspberries and coconut.

tips Substitute papaya or berries for mango, if desired. You will need to cook about ¾ cup of medium-grain white rice for this recipe.

Gluten
FREE

Microwave choc-cherry
SELF-SAUCING PUDDING

PREP & COOK TIME 25 MINUTES **SERVES** 4

- **30g (1 ounce) butter, chopped**
- **¾ cup (110g) self-raising flour**
- **½ cup (110g) caster (superfine) sugar**
- **2 tablespoons cocoa powder**
- **⅔ cup (160ml) milk**
- **½ teaspoon vanilla extract**
- **52g (2-ounce) Cherry Ripe bar, chopped coarsely**
- **¼ cup (55g) firmly packed light brown sugar**
- **2 teaspoons cocoa powder, extra**
- **1 cup (250ml) boiling water**
- **30g (1 ounce) butter, chopped, extra**

1 Melt butter in a deep 1.5-litre (6-cup) microwave-safe dish, in microwave oven on HIGH (100%) about 1 minute.
2 Add sifted flour, caster sugar and cocoa to dish with milk and vanilla; whisk until smooth. Stir in Cherry Ripe.
3 Combine brown sugar and sifted extra cocoa in a medium jug; gradually stir in the boiling water. Add extra butter; stir until butter melts. Carefully pour syrup mixture evenly over the back of a spoon, over pudding mixture.
4 Microwave on HIGH (100%) for 10 minutes or until just cooked in centre. Stand for 5 minutes before serving with cream or ice-cream.

Mini lemon & lime SYRUP CAKES

PREP & COOK TIME 50 MINUTES (PLUS STANDING) **MAKES** 6

125g (4 ounces) butter, chopped

½ cup (110g) caster (superfine) sugar

2 teaspoons finely grated lemon rind

2 eggs

1 cup (150g) self-raising flour

½ cup (125ml) buttermilk

lemon and lime syrup

⅓ cup (80ml) lemon juice

½ cup (110g) caster (superfine) sugar

2 tablespoons water

1 teaspoon long thin strips lemon rind

1 teaspoon long thin strips lime rind

1 tablespoon lime juice

1 Preheat oven to 180°C/350°F. Grease six-hole mini bundt pan or texas (¾-cup/180ml) muffin pan.

2 Beat butter, sugar and rind in a small bowl with an electric mixer until light and fluffy. Add eggs, one at a time. Transfer mixture to a medium bowl; stir in sifted flour and fold in buttermilk.

3 Divide mixture among pan holes, smooth tops. Bake about 25 minutes or until a skewer inserted into centre of cakes comes out clean.

4 Meanwhile, make lemon and lime syrup.

5 Stand cakes in pan 5 minutes before turning onto wire rack over a tray. Pour hot syrup evenly over hot cakes. Serve cakes warm.

lemon and lime syrup Stir lemon juice, sugar and the water in a small saucepan over low heat until sugar dissolves. Bring to the boil. Boil for 1 minute or until thickened slightly. Remove from heat. Strain into a medium heatproof jug. Stir in rind and lime juice.

Cheap
EAT

ALLSPICE also known as pimento or jamaican pepper; so-named because it tastes like a combination of nutmeg, cumin, clove and cinnamon. Available whole (a dark-brown berry the size of a pea) or ground.
ALMONDS flat, pointy-tipped nuts with a pitted brown shell enclosing a creamy white kernel which is covered by a brown skin.
blanched brown skins removed.
flaked paper-thin slices.
BASIL an aromatic herb; there are many types, but the most commonly used is sweet, or common, basil.
BEANS
broad (fava) available dried, fresh, canned and frozen. Fresh should be peeled twice (discarding both the outer long green pod and the beige-green tough inner shell); the frozen beans have had their pods removed but the beige shell still needs removal.
green also known as french or string beans (although the tough string they once had has generally been bred out of them), this long thin fresh bean is consumed in its entirety once cooked.
kidney medium-size red bean, slightly floury in texture yet sweet in flavour; sold dried or canned, it's found in bean mixes and is used in chilli con carne.
sprouts also known as bean shoots; tender new growths of assorted beans and seeds germinated for consumption.
BEETROOT (BEETS) firm, round root vegetable.
BICARBONATE OF SODA (BAKING SODA) a raising agent.
BREADCRUMBS
packaged fine-textured, crunchy, white breadcrumbs.
panko also known as japanese breadcrumbs. They are available in two types: larger pieces and fine crumbs. Both have a lighter texture than Western-style breadcrumbs. They are available from Asian grocery stores and larger supermarkets.
BUCKWHEAT a herb in the same plant family as rhubarb; not a cereal so it is gluten-free. Available as flour; ground (cracked) into coarse, medium or fine granules (kasha) and used similarly to polenta; or groats, the whole kernel sold roasted as a cereal product.
BUTTER use salted or unsalted (sweet) butter; 125g is equal to one stick of butter (4 ounces).
BUTTERMILK originally the term given to the slightly sour liquid left after butter was churned from cream, today it is made from no-fat or low-fat milk to which specific bacterial cultures have been added. Despite its name, it is actually low in fat.
CAPERS grey-green buds of a warm climate shrub (usually Mediterranean); sold dried and salted or pickled in a vinegar brine. Baby capers are very small and have a fuller flavour. Rinse well before using.
CAPSICUM (BELL PEPPER) also called pepper. Comes in many colours: red, green, yellow, orange and purplish-black. Be sure to discard seeds and membranes before use.
CAYENNE PEPPER a long, thin-fleshed, extremely hot red chilli usually sold dried and ground.
CHEESE
brie oft-ripened cow-milk cheese with a delicate, creamy texture and a rich, sweet taste; brie should have a bloomy white rind and creamy, voluptuous centre which becomes runny with ripening.
cream commonly called philadelphia or philly; a soft cow-milk cheese, its fat content ranges from 14 to 33%.
fetta Greek in origin; a crumbly textured goat- or sheep-milk cheese having a sharp, salty taste. Ripened and stored in salted whey; particularly good cubed and tossed into salads.
labne is a soft cheese made by salting plain (natural) yoghurt and draining it of whey for up to 2 days until it becomes thick enough to roll into small balls, which may be sprinkled with or rolled in chopped herbs or spices.
mozzarella soft, spun-curd cheese; originating in southern Italy where it was traditionally made from water-buffalo milk.
parmesan also called parmigiano; is a hard, grainy cow-milk cheese originating in the Parma region of Italy.
pizza a blend of grated mozzarella, cheddar and parmesan cheeses.
ricotta a soft, sweet, moist, white cow-milk cheese with a low fat content (8.5%) and a slightly grainy texture. The name roughly translates as "cooked again" and refers to ricotta's manufacture from a whey that is itself a by-product of other cheese making.
CHICKPEAS (GARBANZO BEANS) an irregularly round, sandy-coloured legume. Has a firm texture even after cooking, a floury mouth-feel and robust nutty flavour; available canned or dried (soak for several hours in cold water before use).
CHORIZO a sausage of Spanish origin; made of coarsely ground pork and highly seasoned with garlic and chilli. They are deeply smoked, very spicy, and are available dry-cured or raw (which needs cooking).
CINNAMON available in pieces (called sticks or quills) and ground into powder; one of the world's most common spices, used as a sweet, fragrant flavouring for both sweet and savoury foods.
COCOA POWDER also known as unsweetened cocoa; cocoa beans (cacao seeds) that have been fermented, roasted, shelled, ground into powder then cleared of most of the fat content.
COCONUT
cream obtained commercially from the first pressing of the coconut flesh alone, without the addition of water; the second pressing (less rich) is sold as coconut milk. Available in cans and cartons at most supermarkets.
desiccated concentrated, dried, unsweetened and finely shredded coconut flesh.
flaked dried flaked coconut flesh.
shredded unsweetened thin strips of dried coconut flesh.
CORIANDER also known as pak chee, cilantro or chinese parsley; a bright-green leafy herb with a pungent flavour. Both stems and roots of coriander are also used in cooking; wash well before using. Also available ground or as seeds; these should not be substituted for fresh coriander as the tastes are completely different.
CORN, PUFFED whole grain corn is steamed until it puffs up.

COUSCOUS a fine, grain-like cereal product made from semolina; from the countries of North Africa. A semolina flour and water dough is sieved then dehydrated to produce minuscule even-sized pellets of couscous; it is rehydrated by steaming or with the addition of a warm liquid and swells to three or four times its original size; eaten like rice with a tagine, as a side dish or salad ingredient.
CRANBERRIES available dried and frozen; have a rich, astringent flavour and can be used in cooking sweet and savoury dishes. The dried version can usually be substituted for or with other dried fruit.
CREAM
pouring also called pure or fresh cream. It contains no additives and has a minimum fat content of 35%.
sour a thick cultured soured cream. Minimum fat content of 35%.
thickened (heavy) a whipping cream that contains a thickener. It has a minimum fat content of 35%.
CUCUMBER, LEBANESE short, slender and thin-skinned. Probably the most popular variety because of its tender, edible skin, tiny, yielding seeds, and sweet, fresh and flavoursome taste.
CUMIN also known as zeera or comino; resembling caraway in size, cumin is the dried seed of a plant related to the parsley family. Available dried as seeds or ground. Black cumin seeds are smaller than standard cumin, and dark brown rather than true black; they are mistakenly confused with kalonji.
DUKKAH an Egyptian specialty spice mixture made up of roasted nuts, seeds and an array of aromatic spices.
EGGPLANT also known as aubergine.
EGGS we use large chicken eggs weighing an average of 60g unless stated otherwise in the recipes in this book. If a recipe calls for raw or barely cooked eggs, exercise caution if there is a salmonella problem in your area, particularly in food eaten by children and pregnant women.
FENNEL also called finocchio or anise; a crunchy green vegetable slightly resembling celery that's eaten raw in salads; fried as an accompaniment; or used as an ingredient in soups and sauces. Also the name given to the dried seeds of the plant which have a stronger licorice flavour.
FILLO PASTRY paper-thin sheets of raw pastry; brush each sheet with oil or melted butter, stack in layers, then cut and fold as directed.
FISH FILLETS, FIRM WHITE blue eye, bream, flathead, snapper, ling, swordfish, whiting, jewfish or sea perch are all good choices. Check for small pieces of bone and use tweezers to remove them.
FLOUR
plain (all-purpose) a general all-purpose wheat flour.
rice very fine, almost powdery, gluten-free flour; made from ground white rice. Used in baking, as a thickener, and in some Asian noodles and desserts. Another variety, made from glutinous sweet rice, is used for chinese dumplings and rice paper.
self-raising plain flour sifted with baking powder in the proportion of 1 cup flour to 2 teaspoons baking powder.
wholemeal also known as wholewheat flour; milled with the wheat germ so is higher in fibre and more nutritional than plain flour.
GARAM MASALA a blend of spices including cardamom, cinnamon, cloves, coriander, fennel and cumin, roasted and ground together. Black pepper and chilli can be added for a hotter version.
GHEE clarified butter; with the milk solids removed, this fat has a high smoking point so can be heated to a high temperature without burning. Used as a cooking medium in Indian recipes.
GINGER, FRESH also called green or root ginger; the thick gnarled root of a tropical plant.
HONEY the variety sold in a squeezable container is not suitable for the recipes in this book.
KUMARA the Polynesian name of an orange-fleshed sweet potato often confused with yam.
LAMB'S TONGUE also called lamb's lettuce, mâche and corn salad, has small, tender, velvety leaves. It is sold in punnets and is available from autumn into spring.
LEMON GRASS a tall, clumping, lemon-smelling and -tasting, sharp-edged grass; the white part of the stem is used, finely chopped, in cooking.
LENTILS (RED, BROWN, YELLOW) dried pulses often identified by and named after their colour; also known as dhal.
LETTUCE
butter (boston) small, round, loosely formed heads with a sweet flavour; soft, buttery-textured leaves range from pale green on the outer leaves to pale yellow-green inner leaves.
cos (romaine) long, with leaves ranging from dark green on the outside to almost white near the core; the leaves have a stiff centre rib giving a slight cupping effect to the leaf on either side.
iceberg a heavy, firm round lettuce with tightly packed leaves and crisp texture.
MAPLE SYRUP also called pure maple syrup; distilled from the sap of sugar maple trees found only in Canada and the USA. Maple-flavoured syrup or pancake syrup is not an adequate substitute for the real thing.
MAYONNAISE, WHOLE-EGG commercial mayonnaise of high quality made with whole eggs and labelled as such; some prepared mayonnaises substitute emulsifiers such as food starch, cellulose gel or other thickeners to achieve the same thick and creamy consistency but never achieve the same rich flavour. Must be refrigerated once opened.
MIXED SPICE a classic spice mixture generally containing caraway, allspice, coriander, cumin, nutmeg and ginger, although cinnamon and other spices can be added. It is used with fruit and in cakes.
OIL
olive made from ripened olives. Extra virgin and virgin are the first and second press, respectively, of the olives; "light" refers to taste not fat levels.
peanut pressed from ground peanuts; most commonly used oil in Asian cooking because of its high smoke point (capacity to handle high heat without burning).
sesame used as a flavouring rather than a cooking medium.
vegetable oils sourced from plant rather than animal fats.

ONIONS
green also known as scallion or, incorrectly, shallot; an immature onion picked before the bulb has formed. Has a long, bright-green edible stalk.
red also known as spanish, red spanish or bermuda onion; a sweet-flavoured, large, purple-red onion.
shallots also called french shallots, golden shallots or eschalots; small, brown-skinned, elongated members of the onion family.
spring have small white bulbs and long, narrow, green-leafed tops.
PAPRIKA ground, dried, sweet red capsicum (bell pepper); there are many types available, including sweet, hot, mild and smoked.
PEPITAS (PUMPKIN SEED KERNELS) are the pale green kernels of dried pumpkin seeds; they can be bought plain or salted.
PINE NUTS not a nut but a small, cream-coloured kernel from pine cones. Toast before use to bring out their flavour.
POLENTA also known as cornmeal; a flour-like cereal made of ground corn (maize). Also the name of the dish made from it.
POMEGRANATE dark-red, leathery-skinned fruit about the size of an orange filled with hundreds of seeds, each wrapped in an edible lucent-crimson pulp with a unique tangy sweet-sour flavour.
PROSCIUTTO a kind of unsmoked Italian ham; salted, air-cured and aged, it is usually eaten uncooked.
QUINOA pronounced keen-wa; is the seed of a leafy plant similar to spinach. It has a delicate, slightly nutty taste and chewy texture.
RICE
arborio small, round grain rice well-suited to absorb a large amount of liquid; the high level of starch makes it especially suitable for risottos, giving the dish its classic creaminess.
basmati a white, fragrant long-grained rice; the grains fluff up beautifully when cooked. It should be washed several times before cooking.
jasmine or Thai jasmine, is a long-grained white rice recognised around the world as having a perfumed aromatic quality; moist in texture, it clings together after cooking. Sometimes substituted for basmati rice.
RICE MALT SYRUP also known as brown rice syrup or rice syrup; is made by cooking brown rice flour with enzymes to break down its starch into sugars from which the water is removed.
ROSEWATER extract made from crushed rose petals; used for its aromatic quality.
SUGAR
brown very soft, finely granulated sugar retaining molasses for its characteristic colour and flavour.
caster also known as superfine or finely granulated table sugar.
icing (confectioners') also known as powdered sugar; pulverised granulated sugar crushed together with a small amount of cornflour (cornstarch).
palm also known as nam tan pip, jaggery, jawa or gula melaka; made from the sap of the sugar palm tree. Light brown to black in colour and usually sold in rock-hard cakes. Substitute with brown sugar if unavailable.
SUMAC a purple-red, astringent spice ground from berries growing on shrubs that flourish wild around the Mediterranean; has a tart, lemony flavour.
TAHINI a rich, sesame-seed paste, used in most Middle-Eastern cuisines, especially Lebanese, in dips and sauces.
TAMARI a thick, dark soy sauce made mainly from soya beans, but without the wheat used in most standard soy sauces.
TAMARIND PUREE (CONCENTRATE) the distillation of tamarind pulp into a condensed, compacted paste. Thick and purple-black, it requires no soaking. Gives a sweet-sour, slightly astringent taste to marinades, pastes, sauces and dressings. Found in Asian food stores.
TOMATOES
canned whole peeled tomatoes in natural juices; available crushed, chopped or diced. Use undrained.
cherry also called tiny tim or tom thumb tomatoes; small and round.
paste triple-concentrated tomato puree used to flavour soups, stews, sauces and casseroles.
roma (egg) these are smallish, oval-shaped tomatoes used in Italian cooking or salads.
TURMERIC related to ginger; adds a golden-yellow colour to food.
VANILLA
bean dried, long, thin pod from a tropical golden orchid; the minuscule black seeds inside the bean impart a luscious flavour in baking and desserts.
extract obtained from vanilla beans infused in water; a non-alcoholic version of essence.
paste made from vanilla beans and contains real seeds. Is highly concentrated: 1 teaspoon replaces a whole vanilla bean. Found in most supermarkets in the baking section.
VINEGAR
apple cider made from fermented apples.
red wine based on fermented red wine.
white wine made from white wine.
WATERCRESS one of the cress family, a large group of peppery greens. Highly perishable, so must be used as soon as possible after purchase. It has an exceptionally high vitamin K content.
WOMBOK (NAPA CABBAGE) also known as chinese cabbage or peking cabbage; elongated in shape with pale green, crinkly leaves, this is the most common cabbage in South-East Asia. Can be shredded or chopped and eaten raw or braised, steamed or stir-fried.
YEAST (DRIED AND FRESH) a raising agent used in dough making. Granular (7g sachets) and fresh compressed (20g blocks) yeast can almost always be substituted for the other.
YOGHURT, GREEK-STYLE plain yoghurt that has been strained in a cloth (muslin) to remove the whey and to give it a creamy consistency.
ZUCCHINI also called courgette; small, pale- or dark-green or yellow vegetable of the squash family.

Conversion chart

Measures

One Australian metric measuring cup holds approximately 250ml; one Australian metric tablespoon holds 20ml; one Australian metric teaspoon holds 5ml.

The difference between one country's measuring cups and another's is within a two- or three-teaspoon variance, and will not affect your cooking results. North America, New Zealand and the United Kingdom use a 15ml tablespoon.

All cup and spoon measurements are level. The most accurate way of measuring dry ingredients is to weigh them. When measuring liquids, use a clear glass or plastic jug with the metric markings.

The imperial measurements used in these recipes are approximate only. Measurements for cake pans are approximate only. Using same-shaped cake pans of a similar size should not affect the outcome of your baking. We measure the inside top of the cake pan to determine sizes.

We use large eggs with an average weight of 60g.

Dry measures

METRIC	IMPERIAL
15G	½OZ
30G	1OZ
60G	2OZ
90G	3OZ
125G	4OZ (¼LB)
155G	5OZ
185G	6OZ
220G	7OZ
250G	8OZ (½LB)
280G	9OZ
315G	10OZ
345G	11OZ
375G	12OZ (¾LB)
410G	13OZ
440G	14OZ
470G	15OZ
500G	16OZ (1LB)
750G	24OZ (1½LB)
1KG	32OZ (2LB)

Liquid measures

METRIC	IMPERIAL
30ML	1 FLUID OZ
60ML	2 FLUID OZ
100ML	3 FLUID OZ
125ML	4 FLUID OZ
150ML	5 FLUID OZ
190ML	6 FLUID OZ
250ML	8 FLUID OZ
300ML	10 FLUID OZ
500ML	16 FLUID OZ
600ML	20 FLUID OZ
1000ML (1 LITRE)	1¾ PINTS

Length measures

METRIC	IMPERIAL
3MM	⅛IN
6MM	¼IN
1CM	½IN
2CM	¾IN
2.5CM	1IN
5CM	2IN
6CM	2½IN
8CM	3IN
10CM	4IN
13CM	5IN
15CM	6IN
18CM	7IN
20CM	8IN
22CM	9IN
25CM	10IN
28CM	11IN
30CM	12IN (1FT)

Oven temperatures

The oven temperatures in this book are for conventional ovens; if you have a fan-forced oven, decrease the temperature by 10-20 degrees.

	°C (CELSIUS)	°F (FAHRENHEIT)
VERY SLOW	120	250
SLOW	150	300
MODERATELY SLOW	160	325
MODERATE	180	350
MODERATELY HOT	200	400
HOT	220	425
VERY HOT	240	475

Index